THE PAGEANT
OF
MEDIEVAL ART AND LIFE

THE PAGEANT OF MEDIEVAL ART AND LIFE

BY
RICHARD McLANATHAN

THE WESTMINSTER PRESS

PHILADELPHIA

PHOTO CREDITS

LIBRARY OF CONGRESS CATALOG CARD No. 66–15817

PUBLISHED BY THE WESTMINSTER PRESS ®
PHILADELPHIA, PENNSYLVANIA
Printed in the United States of America

CONTENTS

FOREWORD

Three great roads converged to form the arts and the culture of the Middle Ages. One was that of the Classic past of Greece and Rome; another, of the exalted mysticism of the Near East; and a third, of the vital tribal traditions of the barbaric north. Though subject to the variety that resulted from constant reinterpretation from time to time and from place to place, these three great ways led to the achievements of the Middle Ages, and when they merged, created the climax of the era in the Gothic flowering expressed in the great cathedrals of the twelfth and thirteenth centuries.

Medieval art, like medieval life, was based on faith. When Constantine the Great adopted Christianity as the religion of the Roman Empire and in 330 established Constantinople as "the Second Rome," a Christian fortress that withstood for a thousand years the onslaughts of Islam, the essential shift took place to mark the ending of the Classic world and the beginning of the emergence of the medieval. There followed an era of great variety and high achievement which drew to its final close in northern Europe in the sixteenth century, a hundred years and more after a new epoch, the Renaissance, had been born in Italy.

The boundaries of the medieval world were those of the old Roman Empire and of Christianity, its inheritor. At their greatest extent, they stretched from the Sahara Desert on the south to the Baltic and the North Seas, from the Atlantic Ocean and the islands offshore, eastward to the Caspian and the Red Seas. But the forces of Islam drove Christianity from its oldest centers in the East, from Antioch and Alexandria, from its very birthplace in the Holy Land itself, leaving civilization divided and embattled. The New World, though reached by far-wandering Vikings, lay remote and unknown, lost beyond miles of stormy seas, even farther from Europe in the Middle Ages than the empire of China, which was visited by such Westerners as Marco Polo, and known as a source of exotic articles of trade.

Our heritage from the Middle Ages is at once broader and deeper than we may know. Such institutions as the United Nations express a concept of world order similar to that underlying the idea of the universal church and the Holy Roman Empire. Our increasing sense of a purpose in life transcending material bounds comes down to us from the Age of Faith. The Middle Ages saw the emergence of languages and literatures, the growth of cities and of business, trade, and technology, the development of hospitals and universities, and the formation of the great national states that today dominate the world scene. The Middle Ages transmitted to later times the traditions of Roman law. It saw man's rights and dignities reaffirmed by the principle of his equality before God, by the exercise of the responsibilities of citizenship that grew in the free cities, and by the growth of the parliamentary system, especially in England during the centuries after a reluctant King John, surrounded by his threatening barons, signed the Magna Carta at Runnymede in 1215.

"The arts," Bernard Berenson once remarked, "embody the hopes and dreams of an era." The arts of the Middle Ages remind us, with poignant power, of a world of grandeur and of hope despite cruelty and suffering, a world infused with purpose and inspired by faith. Through its arts we may gain not only an understanding of an era distant in time but also something of what we have inherited from it and thus increase our knowledge of ourselves in our own times. Man speaks to man through the arts in a language whose idiom and accent may seem strange and different but whose meaning is universal. Thus the arts are a constant reminder of the unity of man, that ideal which has come down to us from the Middle Ages and which we still strive to realize.

I   THE AGE OF FAITH

The Middle Ages have rightly been called the Age of Faith. The story of medieval art is therefore primarily the story of religious art, for religion was so woven into the fabric of life that it pervaded every hour of every day and gave meaning to every thought and experience. The visible world was but a shadow of the perfection that existed in heaven. All of nature was real only as it was symbolic of the true reality that was to be known in the life to come.

Foliage Capitals and Moldings on the Entrance to the Chapter House, Southwell Minster, England, 13th century

Carved Boss in the Vault of Lincoln Cathedral, England, 14th century

In his aspiration toward the divine, man in the Middle Ages thought in symbols. His hopes and fears were expressed by the medieval artist in a language of symbolism that all could read. All sorts of naturalistic elements in his work—birds and squirrels playing in the foliage of a column's capital, a queen petting a puppy in the boss of a cathedral vault, or cats and monkeys sporting in the borders of an illuminated Book of Hours for daily devotion—show the closeness of his observation and his delight in nature. But he was concerned with what was, for him and his age, a higher reality, that of the spirit. Similarity to nature had but little part in his essential purpose. For him it would have been an impious absurdity to make the Virgin look like only a pretty girl. She might be austere and remote, as in the Romanesque period, or smiling and gracious, as in the Gothic, but, above all, she was the Mother of God and the Queen of Heaven whose reign is eternal.

"The Middle Ages," the great French scholar Émile Mâle has observed, "had a passion for order." Men organized their beliefs into the mighty structure of the church. From the Bible, the apocryphal books, and the lives of the saints, the church established a language of symbolism that everyone understood, whatever tongue one

Flight Into Egypt, *Gislebertus, Capital, ca. 1130–1135, Cathedral of Autun, France*

Angel Warning the Magi in a Dream to Avoid the Wrath of Herod, *Gislebertus, Capital, ca. 1130–1135, Cathedral of Autun, France. Archives Photographiques—Paris*

might speak. Many of the symbols were inherited from the pagan past, such as the halo, standing for sanctity. The halo with a cross stood for divinity, and could be used only for God the Father or God the Son. Lilies were Mary's flowers, as they signified her virginity. The blue of her cloak stood for her charity, the red of her dress for her suffering through the death of her Son.

The ass and the ox at the Nativity symbolized the Jews, who had prophesied the coming of the Savior, and the Gentiles, who greeted the birth of Jesus as the fulfillment of the prophecy. The Magi were young, middle-aged, and old to show the three ages of man worshiping Him. Their gifts of gold and frankincense symbolized worldly

Adoration of the Magi, *Gislebertus, Capital, ca. 1130–1135, Cathedral of Autun, France. Archives Photographiques—Paris*

power and heavenly dominion; and myrrh—a
spice that was used in embalming—the death
through which He was ordained to pass to achieve
salvation for mankind. The lamb, the meekest
of creatures and the traditional animal of sacrifice,
was His constant symbol.

Each saint could be recognized by an attribute.
A cosmetic jar, suggesting her formerly frivolous
life, signifies St. Mary Magdalene; an arrow, St.
Sebastian, who was martyred by bowmen; a stone,
St. Stephen, who met death by stoning. A plague
sore and a little dog identify St. Roch, who assisted
those stricken by the Black Death, and was said to
have been fed by his dog when he himself fell ill.
Pilgrims bound for the shrine of St. James wore
the cockleshell that was his symbol. Those who
had been to the Holy Land bore a palm.

The symbolic language of art was thus established. It was the artist's task to interpret the subject in terms of that language. For the less imaginative, this system was a prop and an assistance. The
artist of genius rose above it to invest the familiar
motives with new significance and power. On a
single capital, he could carve the story of the flight
of Joseph and Mary into Egypt with the Christ-
child, or in a series of three, the story of the Magi,
as did Gislebertus in the Cathedral of Autun about
1130, with a narrative technique of clarity and
charm. Or he could show the expulsion of Adam
and Eve from the Garden of Eden, with a force not
to be equaled for centuries, as was done on
the bronze doors ordered by Archbishop Bernẅard
for the Church of St. Michael in Hildesheim, in
northwest Germany, and cast in 1015. He could
use classical restraint, as did the goldsmith Renier
of Huy on the bronze font commissioned about
1108 by Abbot Hellinus for the Church of Notre-
Dame-des-Fonts at Liège in Belgium. On this,
the preaching of St. John and the baptism of Christ
are shown with figures that might almost have
come from an ancient sarcophagus. Or he might
create what has been called the most powerfully
tragic crucifix in the history of sculpture, as did
an unknown master for the Cathedral of Cologne
in about 980.

Like every other epoch in the troubled history of
man, the Middle Ages experienced both triumph
and tragedy. It saw the conflict of faiths between
Christianity and Islam. Internally, within the
body of the church itself, the divisive forces were
at work which shattered its monolithic unity and
made its later division inevitable. Out of the struggle of Christian and Mohammedan, of pope and

Virgin and Child, *School of Auvergne, France, 2d
half of 12th century. The Metropolitan Museum of
Art, New York, Gift of J. Pierpont Morgan, 1916*

emperor, of Byzantine and Goth, and all the welter
of war and destruction gradually emerged the languages and the nations of modern Europe. The
artistic traditions from the Classic past of Greece
and Rome were fused with the elemental expres-
siveness of the barbarian tribes and the intense
mysticism of the Near East, where Christianity
was born to produce the power and the passion of
Romanesque art and the grace and strength of the
Gothic. It was the period of the Crusades and of

Presentation of Christ in the Temple, *Jean Pucelle, from the* Hours of Jeanne d'Evreux, *1325–1328. The Metropolitan Museum of Art, New York, The Cloisters Collection, Purchase, 1954*

pilgrimages, of the founding of universities and the rise of cities. It produced saints as well as warriors, and creators as well as destroyers. Despite violence and discord, it saw artistic achievements of impressive power, from the work of the goldsmith, the ivory carver, the enamelist, and the illuminator of manuscripts to monumental frescoes and great cathedrals.

The Middle Ages believed it the function of the artist to give form to faith. Therefore, whether he produced a manuscript to be seen by only a handful, or sculptures on a church portal to be seen by a multitude, his work could be understood by all. His art was basically an art for everyone, not, as has been the case in later centuries, for the privileged few. Perhaps no artists have striven harder than he to give visible expression to the invisible truths that for him and his age were the essential reality. Through the language of symbolism and allegory he sought, in the words of the great Abbot Suger of St.-Denis, to lead men's thoughts and feelings "from that which is material to that which is immaterial," from the finite to the infinite,

The Expulsion, *from the Bronze Doors of the Church of St. Michael, Hildesheim, Germany, 1015. Hildesheim Cathedral*

The Baptism of Christ, *Renier of Huy, on the Bronze Font for the Church of Notre-Dame-des-Fonts, 1115, Church of St. Barthélemy, Liège, Belgium. Copyright A. C. L., Bruxelles*

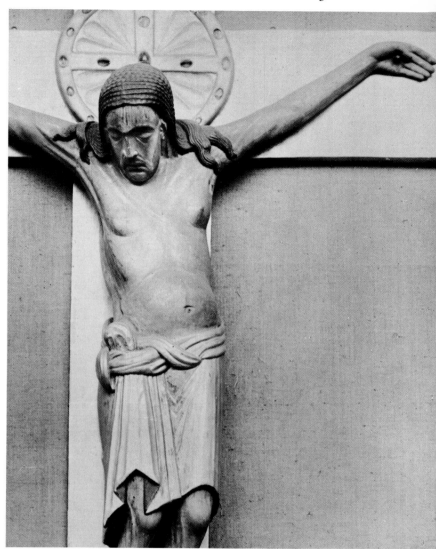

The Gero Crucifix, ca. 980, Cathedral of Cologne, Germany

Detail of the Bronze Font for the Church of Notre-Dame-des-Fonts, Renier of Huy, Liège, Belgium. Copyright A. C. L., Bruxelles

from the momentary to the eternal, from the mundane to the divine.

To understand and to enjoy the art of the Middle Ages, we need not necessarily share all the beliefs of the age that produced it. But through some knowledge of the world in which the medieval artist lived and worked we can better understand the purpose that inspired him, feel his conviction, and admire the power with which he has been able to express thoughts and emotions that lie beyond the scope of forms and words and have become a part of the common hopes and aspirations of mankind.

II CONSTANTINE AND THE TRIUMPH OF CHRISTIANITY

For centuries the imperial throne of Rome had belonged to those who were strong and unscrupulous enough to seize and hold it, and the purple scarcely ever changed hands without being stained in blood. In the year 312 the vast Empire was disrupted by yet another civil war as rival claimants strove for power. Constantine, proclaimed emperor at the distant garrison town of York in the remote and misty northern province of Britain, crossed the Channel and marched south to try to capture the imperial city, held by his rival, Maxentius. As he and his legions moved across Gaul and into Italy they had a vision—as he is later reported to have told a Christian bishop—of a shin-

Portrait of an Unknown Man, *2d century, Catacomb of St. Priscilla, Rome*

ing cross in the sky with the words in fiery letters, *In hoc signo vinces* ("In this sign, conquer").

Constantine's army met the forces of Maxentius outside of Rome. The battle raged all day until the legions from the north, following their standards which bore the strange new symbol of the cross instead of the old pagan sign of the eagle, broke the enemy's lines. Maxentius fled, and in the rout of his army his galloping horse was forced from the Milvian Bridge, which still spans the Tiber north of the city; he drowned in the yellow waters, swollen with the floods of spring. Constantine entered the ancient capital in triumph, and was hailed as emperor by the fickle populace. But his victory did more than provide Rome with a new ruler. It began a new epoch in the world's history. Under his reign a faith that had come from the East a century and a half earlier, and had existed largely as an underground movement among the poor and the downtrodden, became the preferred religion of the Empire. Though paganism lingered long, especially in the north, the old classical world was dying, and the Christian era had begun.

Praying Figure, 2d century, Catacomb of St. Priscilla, Rome

Catacomb of St. Priscilla, Rome. Left, above, Daniel in the Lion's Den; *left, below,* The Sacrifice of Abraham; *2d century*

For some time the old gods had been losing their power as men came increasingly to feel that there must be a deeper meaning to the riddle of life than that which they offered. Mysterious cults arose in the Near East promising more than earthly existence, and seeking identification with the divine through occult ritual and mystic discipline. But it proved to be Christianity that best fulfilled human longing and gave meaning and direction to life.

The early converts to Christianity were mostly simple people—slaves, servants, and freedmen—who met in private houses and in the catacombs, the underground graveyards that honeycombed the countryside outside Rome along the famous roads such as the Appian Way. Too poor to afford the professional artists of the day, they painted somewhat amateurish pictures on the walls behind

Jonah and the Whale, *2d century, Catacomb of St. Callixtus, Rome*

which they buried their dead. These pictures carried a message that the world had never heard before, a message of deliverance from the sin and suffering so much of which they saw around them, especially during the persecutions intended to make them conform to the emperor worship demanded by the Roman state. They used the artistic language and symbols of their own classical

The Miracle of the Multiplication of the Loaves, *2d century, Catacomb of St. Priscilla, Rome*

world, which was their inheritance from the pagan past, to embody the new ideas of a future life beyond death that Christianity promised. Today one may find, deep below the ground on the walls of the narrow passages that wander for miles, many still uncharted, and of the countless chambers that open from them, figures with arms raised in the traditional posture of prayer, standing for the departed soul. To show their faith in Christ's promise of miraculous deliverance, they painted Daniel with the lions, intended by his persecutors to devour him, seated docilely at his side. Noah in his ark,

The Good Shepherd, *3d century, Church of St. John Lateran, Rome*

as small as a skiff, was saved from the terrors of the flood through the same help of God that will save their souls. Jonah, spewed up on shore by the whale, was for them a figuration of deliverance from the misadventures of this world into a life everlasting.

At first the figure of Jesus was never painted. His sufferings were too recent and too sacred. They were not nearly so familiar as the Old Testament stories so well known for so long in the Jewish colonies to be found in every city of the Roman world, and rapidly learned by the many non-Jewish converts to the new faith. Then Christ's miracles began to appear, though without His presence. Artists painted the multiplication of the loaves and fishes to feed the crowds that followed Him to the heights above the Sea of Galilee as a kind of sacramental meal in which the dead person might himself take part, and thus ensure salvation. The healing of the paralytic who took up his bed and walked at Jesus' bidding and the curing of the infirm man at the pool of Bethesda expressed their belief in the power that He would employ also on their behalf.

By about the year 200, Christ Himself begins to appear in art. He is portrayed as a handsome, beardless young man like Apollo or Dionysus, a classical god, but with a great difference, because this figure is a symbol of something beyond the power of the old gods. He appears again and again among the catacomb paintings, with sheep around him, as the good shepherd who "giveth his life for the sheep." In the museum of the famous Roman Church of St. John Lateran, the cathedral of the Pope as Bishop of Rome, there is a third-century statue of Christ as the Good Shepherd. It is the standing figure of a youth in classical costume, carrying a sheep across his shoulders in the same way that shepherds from the beginning of time have carried them, as may still be seen in the remote parts of the British Isles, Spain, Southern Italy, the Balkans, and the Near East. It is thus that Hermes as the shepherd god of the Greeks was represented centuries earlier. In this as in so many other things, not only symbols but also ideas and ideals, the early church borrowed from the past. In the same way, the New Testament became for them the fulfillment of the promises of the Old.

There are a number of representations of Constantine the Great, the first Christian emperor and the victor over Maxentius. The most impressive is the head of a colossal statue that once stood in the basilica which the Emperor completed as a

vast judgment hall in the Roman Forum. Only a few other fragments, including a hand and a foot, remain, but the whole must have stood nearly forty feet high. The head is remarkable for more than its immense size, however, because it is not a portrait in the sense of being a literal physical description of the Emperor's features. It is, rather, a portrayal of the idea of an emperor who was not just an ambitious and opportunistic dictator, like so many of those who had recently preceded him, but a reorganizer and restorer of the Roman state. When compared with the statues of earlier Roman heroes, like Julius Caesar or Augustus, Caesar's grandnephew who was the first emperor, it is clear that the unknown sculptor's and Constantine's ideal was no longer an athletic warrior with a Greek hero's regularity of feature. Instead, though the

The Emperor Constantine the Great, *Capitoline Museum, Rome*

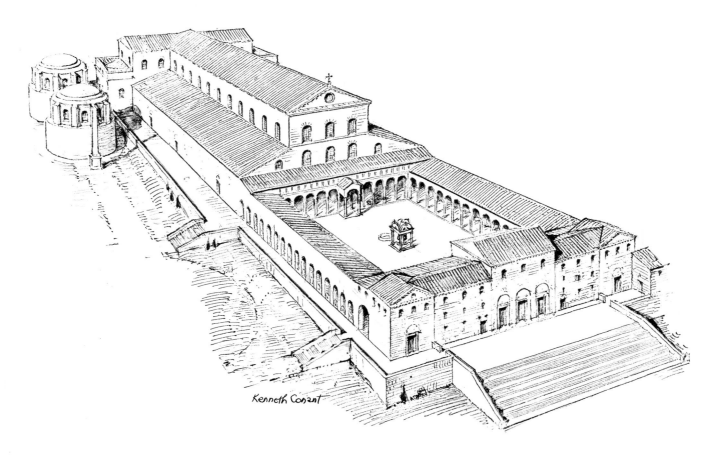

Kenneth Conant

Old St. Peter's, Rome, as of ca. A.D. 600 (Episcopia and fountain, Pope Symmachus, ca. A.D. 500; sanctuary, Pope Gregory I, ca. A.D. 600). Study by K. J. Conant, published by arrangement with the author

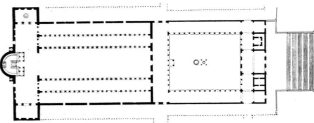

Old St. Peter's, Rome, as of ca. A.D. 600. Drawing by K. J. Conant, published by arrangement with the author

figure was undoubtedly muscular and well proportioned, the heavy chin was Constantine's own, as were the compressed lips and the shape of the nose. But another dimension has been added. The huge eyes, large even for such a colossal head, stare outward in a gaze fixed on a limitless horizon and at the same time suggest the thoughtfulness and the power that lay within. It has become, instead of a superficial likeness, a portrait of imperial power dedicated to an exalted end of Constantine's own envisioning. This sense of otherworldliness and of inner force reflects the new spirit of the times. This spirit was to receive its greatest expression in the Middle Ages, when the inner life and the flame of faith had more intense reality for men than all the varied and fascinating details of the colorful and too often brutal world around them.

Constantine gave generously to the church. He made possible the first great Christian building in the world, and one of the largest churches, Old St. Peter's in Rome, begun in 324 on the site of Nero's circus, where St. Peter himself is believed to have died. The ground plan of the building was larger than a football field. Its immense scale, with a nave as long and as high as the largest Gothic cathedrals, and twice as wide, showed the new imperial importance of Christianity. One ap-

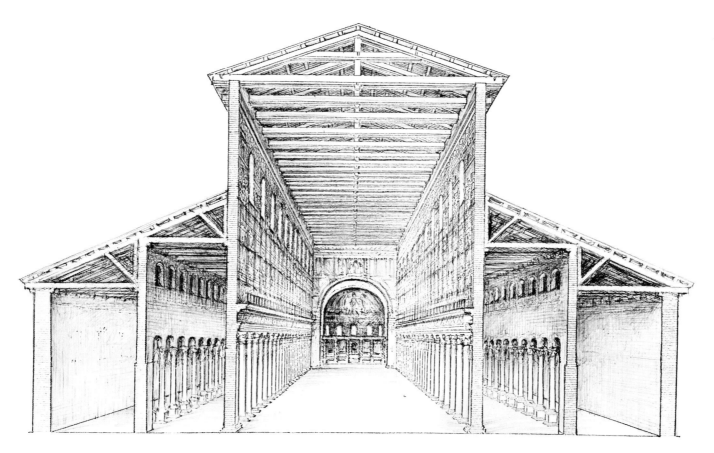

Old St. Peter's, Rome, as of ca. A.D. 600. Study by K. J. Conant, published by arrangement with the author

proached it by mounting a long flight of monumental steps, passing through a triple-arched gateway, crossing a wide, colonnaded court called an atrium after the name for the courtyard of the Roman house from which it was derived and where the early Christian congregations worshiped. Then one entered through one of three great portals into the nave. Far above was the deeply coffered ceiling, painted and gilded. Light coming through the high windows gleamed on walls paneled with rare marbles and decorated with mosaics. It glinted from the gilded capitals of columns, and revealed the richness of the candlesticks and other objects on the high altar three hundred and forty feet away at the far end of the church.

The steady march of the mighty columns on either side of the nave and the rows of tremendous windows high above the elaborate pavement led the eye of the observer along the processional way down the nave and under the triumphal arch that marked the nave's transition into the transept, and finally to the high altar. Beyond was the semicircular apse. Built by the imperial office of works, for what was to become the premier Christian community of the world, Old St. Peter's, dedicated in 326, was large enough to hold half the citizens of

Tomb of Galla Placidia, ca. 450, Ravenna, Italy

the city. It became a place of pilgrimage for people from all parts of the Mediterranean basin as well as from the lands far to the north and east. Its imperial splendor and scale expressed the dream of Roman universality of Constantine and of the early fathers of the church. Just as the earlier artists had borrowed the symbols of the Classic past to adorn the places where they buried their dead in the catacombs, the architects of the cathedral borrowed pagan elements for their plan of the church. They used the long, wide, columned hall, the transept, and the apse of the basilica, and similarly enriched the whole with marbles and mosaics. They put these elements together to serve the requirements of the Christian ritual so successfully that their plan was copied throughout Christendom. For nearly twelve hundred years Old St. Peter's served

the church until, in Renaissance times, instead of carrying out the repairs that the long neglect of its fabric had made necessary, ambitious popes and architects tore it down. It was replaced by the new St. Peter's that we all know. As the Middle Ages waned in the north, St. Peter's was finally crowned with Michelangelo's dome, the one element in the new cathedral that continues the ideal of imperial scale so successfully expressed in Constantine's church of so many centuries before.

Constantine lived long enough to realize many of his aims, but the administration of so vast an empire, with the increasing unrest of the Germanic tribes to the north and east, led him to make a second decision that changed the course of the world's history. In 330 he established a second capital a thousand miles to the east, at Byzantium, at the strategic point where the waters of the Aegean and the Black Seas meet in the Bosporus. Constantinople, as he named it, was a second Rome from which the eastern half of the Empire was to be governed. This fateful decision led eventually to the division of the Empire and the church. When the barbarian tribes of Germany, driven by the Huns — fierce Mongol horsemen from Central Asia — sought lands and treasure in the Roman territories, the western half was overrun. The eastern part remained, though much diminished in extent, to continue the traditions of the Empire and to become the center of the Byzantine style in the arts until its final fall to the Turks in 1453.

During the troubled years of the fourth and fifth centuries the restless barbarian hordes broke through the boundaries of the Empire. They crossed the Rhine and poured into Gaul and Italy, eventually reaching Spain and North Africa. They crossed the Danube to invade Macedonia and Thrace, defeating the imperial armies and penetrating almost to Constantinople itself. Alaric, a chieftain of the West Goths, captured and sacked Rome in 410, and by the middle of the century a West Gothic kingdom extended from central France deep into Spain. The Germans joined the Roman legions against the feared and hated Huns under Attila, "the scourge of God," whom they defeated at Châlons in 451. Before the end of the century, Theodoric, a chieftain of the East Goths, became Emperor of the West. Despite the disturbance of the times, there were those who endeavored to continue the work of Constantine.

The ancient city of Ravenna on the northern shores of the Adriatic became the capital of Italy after the fall of Rome. There Galla Placidia, sister

Interior of the Tomb of Galla Placidia, showing the Mosaic of St. Lawrence

of the Emperor Honorius and wife of a king of the West Goths, built a mausoleum for herself and for the rest of her royal family. It stands today, virtually unchanged since its construction in about 450. Built on the plan of a cross, the outside of the little building is plain to the point of austerity. But in the interior the muted light, filtered through the thin panels of alabaster set into the window frames, creates a mysterious world like that found under the sea. The atmosphere seems to take on the tone of the greenish blue of the mosaics with which the walls and vault are clothed. Above are rosettes, scrolls, and stars, while over the door is the Good Shepherd, seated in a rocky, pastoral landscape. Clad in a robe of imperial purple, He leans on a jeweled cross and extends a hand to one of the several sheep that surround Him, symbols of the Christian souls within His care.

Where the four wings of the building meet, the crossing is domed, with a cupola above. Pairs of white-robed apostles stand between the windows.

The domed ceiling has the cross in the center surrounded by the four signs of the Evangelists, the authors of the four Gospels, the great books of the New Testament: the ox for St. Luke, the lion for St. Mark, the eagle for St. John, and the angel for St. Matthew. Over the altar in the apse is another mosaic, of St. Lawrence carrying a cross and a book and striding to his martyrdom with draperies that flow in folds like the flames licking through the gridiron on which he met his fiery death.

The Romans had had mosaics. They had used them to enrich the pavements of baths and palaces, of temples and villas, from North Africa to Britain. They rarely used them as a wall decoration, preferring paneling with colored marbles or painted scenes from classical mythology. Roman mosaics are made up of small squares of marble in various colors, the range of tone dependent upon the stones used. The Early Christian artists, however, primarily used colored glass for theirs, and usually in smaller cubes. Thus a new world of brilliance

The Good Shepherd, *Mosaic from the Tomb of Galla Placidia*

and color was opened to them. The shiny surfaces of the glass cubes — or tesserae, as they are called — reflected and diffused the light, and created an effect of richness that had never been seen before. The glass could be made in every imaginable shade and tone, and each tessera was individually selected and set in place. Sometimes one can detect as many as twenty or more varieties of gold alone. Their effect was to dissolve the surface of the walls in shimmering light and color, a perfect medium to express the exalted visions of the Christian faith.

Because these artists were representing subjects and figures not of this world, they made no attempt to portray them photographically, but sought a symbolic ideal. Some portrayed Christ as the handsome beardless youth who is the Good Shepherd, and others as thin-faced and dark-bearded as He early appeared in the art of Syria and the East.

Further, these artists were intent upon a reality which they were convinced was so far beyond mundane experience that any attempt at a detailed realism in our sense of the word would merely vulgarize their art and betray its essential message. Their own exaltation is expressed in the serenity and the dignity of the figures of the apostles and the saints, of Christ and the Virgin, and of all the other participants in the divine story. They were not narrating events of momentary significance but were expressing truths they believed to be of everlasting value. Therefore, when the works of these anonymous Early Christian artists are judged according to the genuine standards of all art, in terms of design, fitness, and expression, we recognize their unique achievement, and they speak to us across the years with an eloquence undimmed by time.

Noah, *2d Century, Catacomb of St. Pamfilius, Rome.*

III BYZANTIUM'S GOLDEN AGE

In the year 526, Theodoric the Goth died. Vigorous, unscrupulous, and tolerant, he left a united West to heirs who were unable to maintain their heritage. The next year Justinian, a soldier who was the son of an emperor but the grandson of an Illyrian peasant, ascended the throne of Constantinople to become one of the greatest emperors of either East or West. His brilliant general, Belisarius, conquered the Vandal kingdom of North Africa and left a garrison in Carthage before sailing for Italy. He took Sicily with an amazingly small force, leapfrogged up the coast, and seized Rome, whose inhabitants greeted him with open arms. He successfully withstood siege by the Gothic armies, and took the fight northward into the heart of the enemy's kingdom. The Goths were totally defeated, and those who survived agreed to leave the country. Momentarily the Eastern and Western halves of the Empire were reunited.

But the victory was a disaster for the Italic peoples. The Byzantine forces, split among several campaigns, were too weak, and the Italians were too disorganized to defend the country against the Lombards, a new barbarian horde that swarmed into the peninsula, driven from the Danube frontier by the onslaught of even fiercer Asiatic tribes, during the years following the death of Justinian. By the end of the sixth century they had almost completely overrun it. After several years of senseless massacre and pillage, they finally established their tribal kingdom of semi-independent duchies. They were never able, however, to capture Ravenna or the tip of Southern Italy, both of which remained in Byzantine possession. The Eastern Emperor nominally held sway in Rome also, but the church was divided, and in fact the Bishops of Rome became the rulers of the ancient city. One of them,

Gregory the Great, a Roman aristocrat turned churchman, of the late sixth century, was the first to assume the primacy that the Bishops of Rome have since enjoyed. His claims were much disputed, not only by the Patriarch of Constantinople but also by the other Bishops of equal prestige. So great was the power of Gregory's personality, however, and so vigorous was his policy, that his position foreshadowed the Roman supremacy that eventually emerged. It was he who sent St. Augustine on his famous mission to Christianize England, and his statesmanship resulted in Rome's control of the church in the Frankish kingdoms. He was himself a monk, and his encouragement of monasticism had tremendous importance for civilization and the arts, because the monasteries were outposts and islands of culture in the troubled sea of ignorance and violence that was the world of the earlier Middle Ages.

Thereafter came a long period of disorder in the West. In Italy the invaders gradually began to absorb something of what was left of the civilization they had done so much to destroy. The Frankish kingdoms in the north were in an almost constant state of war. There was continuity in the Eastern Empire, however. Despite the attacks of Germans, Slavs, Bulgars, Persians, and Arabs, Constantinople remained a center of civilization unique in the Occidental world.

Justinian inaugurated what has been called the First Golden Age of Byzantine art because of the rich creativeness of his and succeeding reigns. This may be seen not only in Constantinople but also in works from the other centers of the East, cities that were already ancient when Constantinople was founded—Alexandria, in the delta of the Nile, where Greek artists produced fine ivories;

Antioch, the Syrian city were Christians were first so named; and Jerusalem itself. Today little remains to show their early artistic and religious importance, since almost all traces of their former grandeur were wiped out after their conquest by the Moslems just before the middle of the seventh century. Rome, Ravenna, and Milan were major artistic centers in the West. Artists and craftsmen traveled much, and there was a cross-fertilization among the various centers of East and West. Byzantine influence reached far beyond the immediate Mediterranean world, into the north to the Baltic, and into the east to Armenia, where much was accomplished in art and architecture before these areas were lost in the expansion of Islam. In spite of countless attacks, Constantinople remained a bastion thrust into the often hostile East, a fortress which again and again defended Europe from barbarian hordes, and a cultural center where the Second Golden Age flowered in the ninth century.

Situated on the dividing line between East and

West, the city was at the crossroads of the routes of the world's trade. Camel caravans plodding through the interminable deserts of Central Asia brought silks from the Far East by way of Samarkand and Bokhara. Others carried spices from Arabia, pearls and metalwork from the Persian Gulf, and gold, ivory, and precious stones from East Africa. "Into her harbors," wrote a Byzantine churchman, "sailed expectantly the vessels of the world's trade, and the winds themselves conspired to bring merchandise to enrich her citizens." Thus came furs and hides across the Black Sea from Russia, tin and lead from mines in Portugal and Cornwall, amber from the Baltic, grain and purple dye from North Africa and the Sidonian coast, horses from Spain, wine from Gaul, and silver and asphalt from Palestine. Silks and cottons, aloes, cloves, and sandalwood were shipped from Malaya, China, and the Indies to the great market of Ceylon, from whence Persian merchants shipped them again up the Persian Gulf to the mouths of the Tigris and Euphrates. Or, rounding the Arabian coast into the Gulf of Aden and up the Red Sea, they were carried overland along the route where the Suez Canal was dug centuries later.

The Emperor Justinian with Archbishop Maximianus and Other Attendants, *Mosaic, ca. 547, Church of S. Vitale, Ravenna, Italy*

Merchants, adventurers, and priests brought back tales of their travels to the Isle of Satyrs, which was Borneo with its orangutans, of Indian potentates with their herds of elephants, of giraffes in Africa two stories tall, and of musk deer no larger than a cat. Silk was so sought after by the Emperor and his court that the demand was tremendous and prices consequently high. The Persians made a killing at Byzantine expense until two monks managed to smuggle silkworm eggs, hidden in the hollow of a stick of bamboo, out of China. Syria was soon covered with mulberry trees to supply food for the silkworms. Trade expanded, and the gold coins of the Byzantine Emperor were ready exchange throughout the known world.

Constantinople was the most beautiful city in Christendom, a metropolis of marble palaces, churches, monasteries, universities, spacious squares, and colonnaded streets ornamented with sculptures plundered from captured cities east and west. In its central plaza was the Milestone, a monument from which all distances of the Roman roads were calculated. On a towering column of bronze stood a colossal statue of Justinian on horseback and in full armor, holding the orb of the world,

and resolutely facing to the east, the direction from which came the major threats to the Empire's continuing existence. On one side was the low building with massive gates which was the entrance to the vast enclosure of gardens, groves, churches, and pavilions that formed the Imperial Palace. On another, was the facade of the Senate House, and on a third, Justinian built the great glory of his reign, the Cathedral of St. Sophia.

Nearby was the Hippodrome, where captives and the spoils of war were displayed in triumph, where criminals and enemies of the state were executed, and where the chariot races were held. This sport enlisted such partisan enthusiasm from the populace, which was divided into opposing factions called Greens and Blues, that the loss of a province caused less disappointment than the loss of a race. The crowds cheered their favorites even more passionately than do today's sports fans.

In direct contrast to the violent emotions of the Hippodrome and the teeming life of the streets and quays was the remoteness and dignity of the imperial court. Something of its austere grandeur

The Empress Theodora with Attendants, *Mosaic, ca. 547, Church of S. Vitale, Ravenna, Italy*

Fragment of Mosaic Floor from the Imperial Palace, Constantinople, 6th century

Reliquary of the True Cross, probably made by the Emperor Constantine VII, goldsmith work and cloisonné enamel, 10th century, Limburg an der Lahn, Germany

Detail of the Reliquary of the True Cross, Limburg an der Lahn, Germany

may be seen in the two mosaic panels on either side of the altar in the Church of S. Vitale in Ravenna. One shows the Emperor Justinian, robed in purple, his gold crown set with pearls and seen against a halo to show the divine sanction of his position as head of the Byzantine state. He bears a golden bowl as his offering to the church. With him are courtiers, Archbishop Maximianus with two chanting deacons, and six soldiers, twelve attendants in all, by analogy with Christ and the twelve apostles.

In the other mosaic the Empress Theodora, accompanied by two court officials and seven ladies-in-waiting, brings her offering, a jeweled chalice, to the newly founded church. Symbolically, her purple robe is embroidered with the scene of the Magi bringing their gifts to the Christ-child. Though the heads are clearly portraits of real persons, the whole has been transformed into an abstract imagery to imply the more than human importance of the personages involved. The figures are weightless and suggest by the slight but recurrent rhythm of their poses the ritual formality of the Byzantine court. Their dark eyes stare at us with a compelling gaze suggesting the same inner life that we can see in the great head of Constantine, Justinian's illustrious predecessor.

Delegations coming to Constantinople to visit the Emperor entered the palace grounds through the gates opposite his statue. They were guided by functionaries of the court, who were dressed in embroidered tunics and wore mantles of gold cloth. They passed in a procession between long lines of tall soldiers of the imperial guard with golden shields, silver corselets, helmets of gold with scarlet plumes, and gleaming spears, until they halted before the ivory doors of the audience chamber. The rooms through which they walked were hung with brocades and silken tapestries. The floors, either of marble or mosaic in lively representations of hunting scenes, were covered with Oriental carpets. Finally, after a suitable wait, the ivory doors were opened. With the singing of invisible choirs, a purple curtain was pulled aside to reveal the sacred person of the Emperor. Seated on his golden throne, he was flanked by officers of the guard in white uniforms with gold collars, ceremonially robed senators, and high officials of the court. After a triple prostration of obeisance, the highest ranking of the visitors was permitted to approach across a floor carpeted in rose petals to present his gifts, and then be dismissed with a gracious expression of imperial favor.

The elaborate ceremonial of the Byzantine court existed for a very practical purpose. Many times it so awed threatening barbarians as to discourage their hopes of conquering the master of such wealth and power. All the arts were employed to lend grandeur to the imperial state, including, in the ninth century, those of the most ingenious mechanics in the Western world. Later ambassadors were welcomed by the Emperor seated on a throne that rose above the heads of his courtiers as the visitors approached, while mechanical birds sang in a jeweled tree, mechanical lions roared, griffins opened their beaks and stretched their wings, and a golden organ played.

The palace was not only a treasure-house, however, but also a workshop where silk textiles were woven, enamels and jewels were made, and other precious objects were produced. Most of the finest of these are in the treasury of St. Mark's in Venice. They were taken there as a part of the booty when in 1204 the armies of the Fourth Crusade were prevailed upon by the wily Venetians, jealous of the prosperity of their rivals in the Eastern trade, to capture and sack the ancient Christian city instead of turning their forces against the Saracens. But one of these precious objects, a reliquary with superb cloisonné enamel, became a part of the

St. Michael the Archangel, *leaf of a Diptych, early 6th century, Ivory, 17″ × 1½″. The British Museum, London*

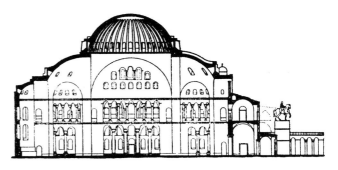

Section of St. Sophia

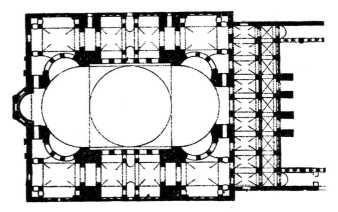

Plan of St. Sophia

Cathedral of St. Sophia, Istanbul, 532–537. The Four Minarets and Surrounding Buildings are Later Turkish Additions

treasure of a German monastery. It was made by an emperor, Constantine VII (913–959), for a fragment of the True Cross, and inscribed with his name. The reliquary's cover is of gold, with a border studded with precious stones. In the center, in nine compartments framed in rows of rubies, are enameled plaques of the twelve apostles, six above and six below, two to a panel. In the three central panels are Christ enthroned, flanked by John the Baptist on the left and the Virgin on the right, each accompanied by an angel as elaborately robed as an official in the imperial court.

Byzantine artistic influence was spread through the multiplicity of such small objects that were sent, carried, stolen, and by one means or another, found their way to the far parts of the known world. There were caskets of ivory and gold, enamel work, chalices, reliquaries, pyxes to hold the host, and other ecclesiastical objects, illuminated manuscripts, and small reliefs in metal and ivory. It was customary for the nobility of the Eastern Empire to commemorate special occasions such as a marriage, the conferring of a consulship, or some other honor, by commissioning ivory carvings. These usually took the form of a diptych, two thin, sculptured panels hinged together, while the small portable altars, known as triptychs because they were made up of three panels, were also objects of rare value. One of the finest remaining of these panels is a relief seventeen inches high preserved in the British Museum. Carved early in the sixth century, shortly before Justinian came to power, it shows the Archangel Michael, holding in his right hand

Cathedral of St. Sophia, Interior

Christ, the Virgin, and St. John, Mosaic, probably after 1150, Cathedral of St. Sophia

the orb surmounted by a cross, signifying Christ's dominion of the world, and in the left, a tall staff of office. He stands against a classical niche, and his draperies swirl in graceful folds reminiscent of a Greek or Roman statue, but his winged body seems to float. The familiar classical harmonies of sculptural form are used to express the spiritualized ideal of the Byzantine Christian world.

Of all the arts none lent more grandeur to the Byzantine tradition than architecture. The single greatest artistic achievement of Byzantium's long history is Justinian's St. Sophia, the Church of the Holy Wisdom. The cornerstone was laid by the Emperor himself in 532, and the building, for centuries the largest vaulted structure in the world, was completed in only five years. It was designed by Anthemius of Tralles and Isidorus of Miletus, two architects from Asia Minor, where for more than a century churches of progressively important construction had been built. Instead of the wooden roof of Old St. Peter's, St. Sophia is vaulted throughout, and instead of having a nave with two aisles on each side, it has a broad, oval central space with single aisles separated by colonnades. The entire emphasis of the design of St. Peter's was on a processional movement toward the single focus of the high altar. In St. Sophia the focus on the altar is balanced by the central emphasis provided by the great dome to which all the elements of the building triumphantly rise. In its combination of the tradition of vaulted construction of the earlier Empire with the domed architecture that had recently been developed in Asia Minor, it is a revolutionary synthesis of East and West.

St. Sophia was turned into a mosque by the Turks after their capture of Constantinople in the fifteenth century. Later its four minarets were built. Its superb mosaics were plastered and whitewashed over, its entrance court destroyed, and its altar, screen, and treasure pillaged. But Moslem architects took it as a model and copied it in several mosques. In recent time it was made into a museum, and American scholars have uncovered many of the mosaics, so that once more one can know something of its former grandeur.

One approached the cathedral through a broad, cloistered court adorned with fountains and sculptures, walked beneath the shadowed narthex or vestibule, then through any of the nine great doors except the central one, which was reserved for the Emperor and the Patriarch, and into the soaring space of the church rising to the dome, 107 feet in diameter, 180 feet above. Because of the ring of closely spaced windows at its base, the dome appears unbelievably light, "hung from the sky," in the words of a contemporary observer. On either side of the hovering dome, half domes descend in graceful curves that never lose their tautness. The light from the many windows pours into the church, to be reflected from the glowing mosaics with the gold backgrounds, and enlivens the many-colored marbles of the walls. The wonderful pavement was like "swirling seas of marble, streaked with deep green or glowing red, powdered with gold stars, or splashed with milky streams on glittering black, or 'like blue cornflowers in grass, with here and there a drift of fallen snow.'"

In the upper arcades that run along the sides of the church the ladies of the court were discreetly protected from curious gaze by delicate latticed grills. A tremendous silver screen, decorated with figures of martyrs and with pairs of winged guardian angels, shut off, according to the traditions of the

Cathedral of St. Mark, Venice, begun 1063

Eastern Church, the altar in the sanctuary, the center of the three apses at the east end. The altar itself was of solid gold, hung with elaborately worked silken curtains, and surmounted by a silver ciborium, or canopy, rising in a gleaming pyramid high above. Behind were the seats for the clergy, curving to meet the throne of the Patriarch in the center of the semicircular apse. The throne was also made of silver and bore reliefs and statuettes of episodes from Scripture, of saints and angels, and of heroes of the Old Testament and the New.

Throughout the long centuries of Byzantine history, St. Sophia continued to be enriched and embellished with mosaics, the most important art form in the East next to architecture. The finest of all are in the south gallery, a figure of Christ in the center, with the Virgin to the left and St. John the Baptist to the right. Despite their fragmentary condition, enough remains so that there can be no doubt of their superb quality. The tiny tesserae have never been set with greater subtlety and the grand scale has never been kept more consistently than here. Made sometime after 1150, the figures have a brooding sadness and quiet dignity. Christ is the judge but His hand is lifted in blessing, and all three seem to share in sympathy the sorrows of a disrupted and suffering world.

The vestments of the Byzantine clergy were of an unbelievable richness. When there was a service at night, attended by crowds of worshipers, with the nobility robed in silks of many hues, the church was a glow of color under the lights of hundreds of perfumed lamps in the form of crowns or

ships of silver and gold hung in clusters like stars far above. The whole cathedral became a tremendous lantern radiating light through countless windows so that it was a beacon for the ships coming up the Hellespont on their way to port. In the light of the lamps one could see the immense mosaics of the four archangels filling the pendentives, the great curving triangles that form the transition between the dome and the four massive piers that rise "like sheer cliffs" from the pavement. The light gleamed on the other mosaics in the apses and the semidomes, on the gilded capitals of the columns of the arcades and the galleries above, and shone on the altar screen and the gold of the Patriarch's crown.

It was to such a nighttime service that a later emperor took the envoys of Vladimir, Great Prince of Kiev, late in the tenth century. "We knew not whether we were in heaven or on earth," they reported to their master on their return, "for on earth there is no such splendor or such beauty." It was thus that Vladimir, a descendant of Vikings, was converted from paganism to the Christianity of the Eastern Empire. The traditions and arts of the Greek Orthodox Church became a part of Russian civilization, and Moscow came to be called the "third Rome."

Just as the serene dome of St. Sophia rose above

Interior of Cathedral of St. Mark, Venice

Cathedral of St. Basil, Moscow, 1554–1560

the city of Constantinople, Byzantine culture and art dominated a vast area of the medieval world, in the Slavic north, and in the churches built all around the Mediterranean shores, but especially in Sicily, Southern Italy, and along the Adriatic. Ravenna became a Byzantine city as the capital of the exarchs who governed the Emperor's Italian domain in his name. So did Palermo in Sicily, where Eastern influence remained strong through all the many conquests by Goths and Vandals, Normans and Arabs. But there is no greater Byzantine monument anywhere outside of Constantinople than the great Cathedral of St. Mark in Venice, begun in 1063.

The city was founded on sandbars off the northwest Adriatic coast by refugees from the Lombard invaders in the middle of the fifth century. It began with clusters of fishermen's huts on piles driven in the mud, but it gradually grew to outrival Byzantium itself in richness and power based on trade between East and West. Palaces and churches rose above the quiet waters of the lagoon. Venetian merchantmen plied the oceans of the world. Venetian galleys, with oars manned by slaves captured in war, not only guarded the city

but kept the peace throughout the greater part of the Mediterranean for centuries. The influence of the Orient appeared in the richness of the robes worn by the Doges, the rulers elected by the council of leading families from among their own number. It appeared also in the constant intrigue of a court so similar in many ways to that of Constantinople, in the spies and informers set by the council to watch their own duke. It was to be seen in the Eastern splendor of Venetian ritual and Venetian architecture, culminating in St. Mark's, beside the Palace of the Doges on the great central square of the city of which it remains the heart.

The plan of St. Mark's is that of a cross within a rectangle, with a central dome and four others covering the arms of the cross, patterned after Justinian's Church of the Holy Apostles in Constantinople. From across the long square of S. Marco, the domes rise in a picturesque profile above the facade, ornamented with mosaics. The four gilt bronze horses of St. Mark, original Greek works of the period of Alexander the Great that were brought to Venice as booty from a successful raid, forever prance above the main portal.

From the brilliant sunlit pavements of the square, one enters a shadowy interior, with subdued light gleaming from the gold grounds of the mosaics that cover the walls and vault. There is none of the Greek clarity of the interior of St. Sophia. Here one cavernous domed area leads into another; chapels are divided from one another and from the main interior by pierced screens of marble with rich inlays. Candles flicker in the perpetual twilight, and chanting voices echo and reecho through an atmosphere fragrant with incense. The air of mystery is Oriental, and shows how completely the influence of the East had come to dominate the Byzantine world of the eleventh and twelfth centuries. The stolen treasures from Constantinople look quite at home there, and the Latin vestments and ritual seem curiously out of place.

The Byzantine style continued in the East following its own patterns of evolution during the periods when the West was struggling to recover from the long disruptions of the Germanic invasions, and achieved the flowering of art that we call the Romanesque because of its harking back, as if to an almost forgotten memory, to the splendors of ancient Rome. The Byzantine style continued through the subsequent period that saw the highest achievements of the Middle Ages, the construction of the great Gothic cathedrals. Byzantine ivories and enamels found their way to the outermost

Old Testament Trinity, *ca. 1410, Andrei Rublev, Panel, 55½″ × 44½″. Tretyakov Gallery, Moscow*

corners of Europe and into the East. Byzantine manuscripts were among the prized possessions of monasteries and provided inspiration for illuminators and sculptors. The five-domed Byzantine church may be found from Périgueux in France to Trebizond in Armenia, from the upper reaches of the Nile north to Russia. But nowhere did it assume a more exotic form than in the famous Church of St. Basil in Moscow.

Dating from 1554, St. Basil's was built during the reign of Ivan the Terrible and displays in its style all the wild extravagance of that mad tyrant. It is less a building than a great pile of masonry that seems to have been hollowed out in a series of small, dark chambers, curiously connected by narrow corridors, and at different levels, the largest of which can hold but a handful of people. But its exterior is what makes it the single most picturesque example of Slavic exuberance. The walls are covered with brightly painted decoration in relief. The steep gables multiply above, until the whole church explodes in a series of spiral or fluted cupolas each crowned by a turnip-shaped dome typical of the Slavic Christian style. Far in the cold north, beside the brooding, sinister, red-walled Kremlin, it represents a passionate and barbaric expression of faith, a cry of protest against the bleakness and cruelty of Slavic despotism,

whose tyranny enslaved both tyrant and subjects alike. It remains a curiously moving and impressive monument to pious hope in a violent past still remaining in a godless present.

Art reached its aesthetic height in Russia in painting, in the work of Andrei Rublev (ca. 1370–1430). His early years were spent as a lay brother in a monastery, where he was apprenticed to an icon painter. The great influence on his life was Theophanes the Greek, an extraordinary artist trained in the traditions of Constantinople, who did both murals and icons in Russia. From him Rublev learned the abstract dignity of the Byzantine style developed over the centuries as a means of expressing faith and spirit rather than describing, as Western art was even then coming to do, the external appearances of things. Never has the otherworldliness of the Byzantine had such delicacy and grace, such rhythmic composition, or such a distinctive coloring of soft greens, blues, and gold as in the work of Rublev.

His greatest single achievement is the *Old Testament Trinity*, painted about 1410 for the monastery of the Trinity and St. Sergius near Moscow, and now in the Tretyakov Gallery in that city. The three graceful and serious angels that visited Abraham and foretold the coming of Christ have long been considered as a prefiguration of the Trinity, the threefold nature of God as Christ, the Holy Spirit, and eternal Father. The similarity of the three angels to one another suggests that the three are one, as does the composition that links them by subtly flowing lines. The soft color and the flame-like forms become an expression of the quiet, mystic rapture of a man who had lived through the violence of Tartar invasions and the dread uncertainties and cruelties of Czarist despotism with faith unquenched.

The Byzantine tradition continued even after the final and irrevocable capture of Constantinople by the Turks in 1453, when the early Renaissance was in full flood in Italy. It remains alive today in such refuges as the fantastic cliff-top monasteries of Mt. Athos in eastern Greece, where the monks still paint icons according to the style and formula of a centuries-old past. It exists also in the ritual of the Eastern Church, with its Greek liturgy and gold-crowned priests, which, despite persecution, still lives on to suggest, along with the few remaining churches and monasteries, ivories, manuscripts, goldsmith work, and rich textiles preserved in cathedral treasuries and museums, the splendors and triumphs of a great past.

IV THE WORLD OF ISLAM

In 604, while the indomitable Gregory the Great, "Servant of the servants of God," lay dying in Rome, a young Arab was having visions in distant Mecca that were to change the course of history. The young man was Mohammed, a successful trader in a community that was a business as well as a religious center. There goods from far and near were bartered. And there, from all over the Arab world, countless people congregated for the annual Hajj, a pilgrimage and festival that centered about a mysterious black meteorite set in the wall of a shrine called the Kaaba which had been the object of worship from time out of mind.

Arab religion was a matter of primitive awe of pillars and places, of inherited ritual whose purpose and meaning had long since been forgotten. Christianity and Judaism had both penetrated the Arab world, however, and profoundly influenced Mohammed's ecstatic visions, which he believed he had received directly from the Archangel Gabriel. Gradually his incoherent and wild messages took on the pattern of a profession of faith in Allah, the one god, "the Lord of the worlds, the merciful, the compassionate." Mohammed saw himself as the last of a line of true prophets including Abraham, Moses, and Jesus.

At first Mohammed was scorned, but he gradually gained a small, fanatic following of men who were fired by his passionate sermons full of half-understood fragments of Scripture and of Jewish and Christian tradition. Out of these sermons emerged certain central ideas that had a compelling simplicity as compared with the threats of the vengeful and jealous deity of the Jews and the hair-splitting, cantankerous dogmatism of the Christians, with their disputes and persecutions. He exhorted his followers to feed their slaves "with such food as ye eat yourselves, and clothe them with the stuff that ye wear," to "treat your women well . . . . Ye have verily taken them on security of God, and have made their persons lawful to you by the words of God." But above all, he preached that "every Moslem is the brother of every other Moslem. All of you are of the same equality." These were things that the illiterate and semi-barbarous Bedouin could understand, beliefs that he could make a part of the pattern of his life.

In 622, Mohammed's preaching had become so inflammatory and objectionable to the conservative Arab community that he fled for his life to Medina, another Arab city about two hundred miles due north. This event, called the Hejira, or migration, was the turning point. It is from that date that his followers reckon the start of their calendar.

Mohammed grew in power, and the number multiplied of those who embraced Islam ("submission," in Arabic), because they submitted to the will of Allah as interpreted by Mohammed as his Prophet. He led attacks on the caravans from Mecca, thus gaining necessary funds and at the same time wreaking the vengeance of Allah on the unbelievers. His successful raids drew more followers, and in 630 he returned to Mecca in triumph, having convinced the Arabs of the Hedjaz of the truth of his teaching by force of arms when exhortation had failed. For the first time in history a unifying force had emerged among the Arab tribes.

Mohammed died two years later, and a struggle for power among his followers was solved by violence. The strongest and most ruthless prevailed, and Islam was unleashed as a new force. Arab horsemen swept into Iraq and Syria, invaded the ancient dominions of Persia, weakened by years of war with Byzantium, and into Byzantine territories, which the exhausted imperial troops could no longer defend. The great centers of civilization fell before the Moslem horde, Acre, Tyre, and Sidon, and then Jerusalem and Antioch. Further waves flowed eastward to Samarkand and the Hindu Kush. Early in the eighth century, Arab cavalry took Turkistan and invaded China, only to be finally repulsed by desperate efforts of Chinese arms. But the Arab empire held northwest India and the passes of the Pamir.

In the West, Egypt fell and Old Cairo was established as the new Arab capital. When the fierce Berbers of the mountains of North Africa were converted, the entire southern shore of the Mediterranean was overrun, and Spain and Sicily were invaded. The northward drive of Moslem power was finally stopped only on the banks of the Loire by the Franks under Charles the Hammer in a great battle near Tours in 732. Meanwhile Arab fleets dominated much of the Mediterranean. Moslem corsairs harried the shores of Greece and Italy. They were prevented from taking Constantinople itself only by the courage and military genius of the Emperor Leo in 717, when the terrors of Greek fire, for centuries a secret weapon of the Byzantines, routed the Saracen fleet.

In the eleventh century a new wave of Asiatic barbarians swept in from the East, the Seljuk Turks, who appreciated Arab civilization as little as Christian. But they too were converted to Islam, and before the end of the century had carried the green banner of the Prophet to the very gates of Constantinople. The Crusades turned the tide. The Christian wall held, based on Byzantium, until the Mongol horsemen of Genghis Khan rode down from the steppes in the thirteenth century. The Ottoman Turks invaded the Balkans in the fourteenth, overran the lands of the Seljuks, and finally, in 1453, after the close of the Middle Ages, captured the ancient stronghold of Christendom. The last emperor, Constantine XIII, died a hero's death fighting to the end. But for more than a thousand years Constantinople had held the Eastern frontier, and not only saved the heritage of Western culture but made possible the flowering of medieval Europe.

Islamic civilization, a combination of borrowings from the many peoples that were conquered by the Mohammedans, contains elements from Persians and Mongols, and from North Africa and Spain, as well as from the Classic Mediterranean

Interior of the Mosque of Cordova, Spain, 785–987

past of Greece and Rome. Islamic art is characterized by brilliant color and rich decoration in complex patterns based on the sinuous, curving line that has come to be known as the arabesque. Like all peoples of nomadic origin, the tribes that made up the Islamic world loved sumptuous objects that were portable, such as rugs, pottery, and metalwork. Even today an Arab merchant taking passage on a dhow from the shores of the Persian Gulf or the Red Sea to the Hadramaut, to the east coast of Africa, or to India carries his own carpets and utensils, including vases for flowers as well as dishes for serving the food that he also supplies himself.

The culture of the Arabs was vastly inferior to that of the countries they subjected. After initial pillage and destruction they recognized the wisdom of allowing the subject populations to continue in their traditional pursuits so long as their tribute continued also. Christians went on worshiping in their churches, and Jews in their synagogues. The luxuries of Byzantine life appealed to a people who had lived for centuries in the hostile desert. The genius of Byzantine architects and artists was employed to build mosques and palaces and embellish them with marbles and mosaics. Imperial administration methods were borrowed to govern the far-flung territories of the Arab domain.

As the power of the Arab world grew, its leadership was disputed. A series of states emerged, each under a separate emir, in Spain, North Africa, Egypt, and Asia Minor, but all were united by a similar language and acknowledged the religious leadership of the caliph as the successor to Mohammed. The Koran, the collection of Mohammed's messages to his followers, was the sacred book that contained the beliefs and laws of life of the Moslems. Five times a day, then as now, all Mohammedans turned toward Mecca to the same call to prayer that was cried by muezzins from minarets from Spain to the Punjab. All dreamed of the pilgrimage to Mecca, the culmination of earthly life for devout followers of the Prophet.

Mohammed himself had been a merchant. The Arabs' conquest gave them control of the trade routes from Africa and the East. They took full advantage of it, and trade flourished throughout the Moslem world. Arab merchants established themselves as far away as China and India, and there came to be a lively exchange between Saracen and Christian merchants in Constantinople and elsewhere. Turbaned Arab delegations were seen in Pisa, Venice, Naples, and Amalfi. Desert simplicity gave way to a taste for luxury that rivaled

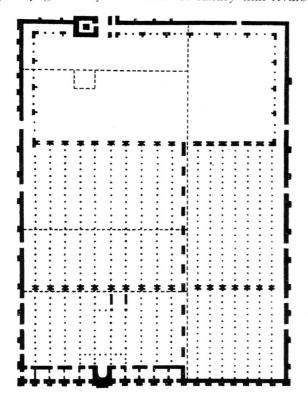

Plan of the Mosque of Cordova

Byzantium at its most opulent, and all the skills of architect, artist, and artisan went to satisfy the restless appetite for splendor of the Arab sovereigns. Cities were founded. There was no limit to the extent to which the absolute rulers poured out treasure to glorify their reigns by splendid buildings.

The Great Mosque of Damascus, now a ruin, was decorated with mosaics by Byzantine artists. That at Samarra, northwest of Baghdad, built in the middle of the ninth century, had a ground plan almost ten acres in extent, of which more than half was covered by a wooden roof supported by a forest of columns. It has long since fallen into ruin. Only its walls and minaret with spiral ramp remain. But the appearance of its interior may be seen by visiting the Mosque of Cordova in Spain, begun in 785 by Abdurrahman I and further enlarged in the ninth and tenth centuries, to become the center of Moslem power in the West. In every direction the vast interior extends in an ever-changing perspective of innumerable columns of porphyry, jasper, and marble, many taken from the old Visigothic cathedral. There are no alternations of interval, as between the nave and aisles of a church, but merely the march of columns, row upon row, leading eastward, in the direction of Mecca. It is like walking through a carefully planted grove of hundreds of petrified trees, shadowed from the brilliant sun of the walled courtyard outside, mysterious and apparently endless. Nothing could be more unlike the concept of architectural space of the Early Christians and the Byzantines than this, whose bounds are deliberately obscured to suggest a mystery of limitless extent.

Just as Mohammed borrowed features from both Judaism and Christianity to form Islam, so the Moslem architects borrowed towers from early churches in Syria for minarets. They took the horseshoe arch from the earlier Near East, mosaics from Byzantium, the dome from Constantinople, and wood carving from Coptic Egypt. The rich patterns of Persian textiles were imitated in tile, wood, brick, and stone. Masons and other artisans of all nationalities were employed for the greater glory of Allah and the caliphs.

In the same way Arab scholars borrowed the learning of Greece from Byzantium. They translated into Arabic the classical texts on science and mathematics, on medicine by Galen and Dioscorides, on mechanics by Archimedes, the astronomy of Ptolemy, and the monumental works of Aristotle in which he attempted to organize and codify the learning of the ancient world. An Arab Renaissance

Physicians Preparing Medicine, *from an Arabic Translation by Abdallah ibn al-Fadl of the* Materia Medica *of Dioscorides, 1224.* Freer Gallery of Art, Washington, D.C.

resulted in the ninth, tenth, and eleventh centuries. Great universities were founded, such as that at Cordova in Spain, where students congregated from all parts of the Moslem world and beyond. Thus when there was a period of darkness and ignorance in the West, Arab curiosity and scholarship not only kept alive the heritage of the Classic past but made contributions to knowledge in science, medicine, and engineering. The first introduction of many a later Western scholar to the learning of Greece was through an Arab translation.

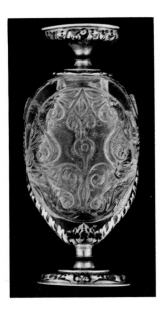

Egyptian Glass Goblet, 10th century. Freer Gallery of Art, Washington, D.C.

Like Judaism, Islam theoretically forbids the representation of human or animal figures. Actually the prohibition was applied only to things of large scale, such as public monuments. Things too small to cast a shadow were considered acceptable. Thus figures appear in rugs, on pottery, and on other objects of domestic use, and in Persian miniatures of the fourteenth and fifteenth centuries, which are among the most brilliant achievements of Islamic art. Full of liveliness and verve, they show heroic warriors battling to the death, kings and princes hawking and hunting in ideal land-

Hunting Scene, *from a Persian Manuscript of a Poem by Nizāmī, Shīrāz, 1548. Freer Gallery of Art, Washington, D.C.*

Coronation Robe of the Holy Roman Emperors, made in Sicily for Roger II, 1133–1134, red silk embroidered in gold. Kunsthistorisches Museum, Vienna

scapes, or meeting beautiful princesses in palace courts or gardens whose fanciful charm owes much to the Far East.

Islamic textiles, silks woven in patterns of birds or lions or fabulous beasts, rivaled the products of the looms of Byzantium and the Far Orient. They were used for royal robes and priestly vestments, and are often found in the treasuries of European cathedrals. Islamic craftsmanship was much admired for its Oriental intricacy, and objects in glass and metalwork were similarly prized. They were imported by Western merchants, or along with carpets, taken back as booty by the Crusaders, and Persian glass goblets served as chalices in Christian churches.

The superb coronation robe of the Holy Roman Emperors was embroidered by Islamic craftsmen in twelfth-century Palermo for the Norman King of Sicily, Roger II. On either side of the tree of life, fantastic lions attack camels in a design that goes back to the very beginnings of Eastern art. They are so stylized that at first glance one hardly recognizes the forms of the animals at all, yet they are full of vigor. In this abstract quality the essence of the Islamic sense of design emerges most strongly. Though Moslem artists occasionally created a figural art of superb quality, as in the

Persian miniatures, their basic reluctance to represent figures led them to create a nonrepresentational style of great distinction.

Like the Chinese and the Japanese, who may have influenced them in this regard, the Moslems developed calligraphy into a fine art. The pages of their manuscripts, especially of the Koran, exploit all the decorative possibilities of the Arabic script to become wonders of subtle, sinuous design,

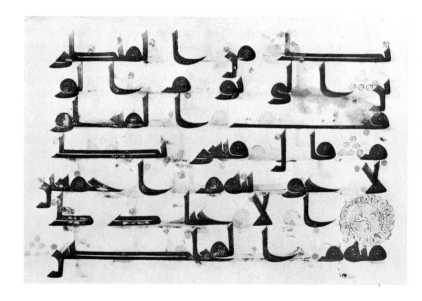

A Page from the Koran, Egypt, 9th century. Freer Gallery of Art, Washington, D.C.

Taj Mahal, Agra, India, 1630–1648

beautiful and expressive in themselves whether one can read Arabic or not. Pious inscriptions in monumental size assume the importance on the wall of mosque or tomb of mosaic friezes in Byzantian churches.

Many of the greatest achievements of Islamic art, such as the famous Taj Mahal in Agra, India, and the Mosque of Ahmed I in Istanbul, both of the seventeenth century, came long after the end of the Middle Ages in Europe. But the caliphs of Cordova began early in the tenth century to transform Andalusia, a district of high, bare mountains and fertile valleys in southern Spain, into a place of gardens, villas, and palaces so beautiful that for generations of Arabs it was a promised land. The three great cities of Andalusia—Cordova, Seville, and Granada—were among the most flourishing in the Moslem empire. In appearance Cordova is an Oriental city with narrow, winding streets and whitewashed walls with few windows. The houses and palaces look inward in Eastern fashion, guarding their secrets from the outside world as in Moslem cities from Marrakech to Baghdad. Yet little remains intact from Saracen times except the great mosque, now the cathedral, with its broad court with five fountains, and rows of orange trees so like the ranks of columns within the shadowy interior.

The Cathedral of Seville, seventy-five miles down the valley of the Guadalquivir, still has a similar Moorish court. It also boasts what many have long considered the most beautiful Islamic tower in the world, though there are others similar to it in Marrakech and Rabat in North Africa. The tower is called the Giralda (weather vane in Spanish) because of the statue that turns in the wind placed on top of it in the sixteenth century. It was a part of the twelfth-century mosque built by Ahmed Benbasso, and is so large that it may be climbed by a ramp wide enough for two horsemen to ride abreast. Originally it was surmounted by four immense copper globes, gilded to shine in the sun, but in 1568 a five-storied bell tower was built on top of it in a fanciful Spanish style that reflects such strong Islamic influence that it seems perfectly in keeping. Even without this addition the Giralda combined Christian and Moslem elements. The windows have both Arab and Visigothic capitals. The latter were taken from the Visigothic cathedral that was demolished to make way for the mosque, just as the mosque in its turn was replaced by the present cathedral which is, next to St. Peter's in Rome, the largest in

Mosque of Ahmed I, Istanbul, 1609–1616

the world. This interchange and combination of Eastern and Western elements is typical of the art of Spain during the Middle Ages as in later centuries as well.

After the fall of the caliphate to Christian armies, the city of Granada, in the midst of rugged mountains, was the capital of a Moorish kingdom. This last stronghold of the Arabs in Spain was finally reconquered by the soldiers of Ferdinand and Isabella in the same year that Columbus sailed on his momentous voyage. There Islamic art in the West reached a fanciful climax in the famous palace of the Alhambra, begun in the thirteenth century by Mohammed I, friend of St. Ferdinand, King of Aragon. Above the city, against the snowcapped peaks of the Sierra Nevada far beyond, rise the walls and towers of the palace. It is built on an outthrust shoulder of the hillside high above the remains of the old Arab city and the steep valley whose whitewashed caves for centuries have been inhabited by Gypsies. On a yet higher shoulder the dark green of thickly clustered cypresses shows the location of the Generalife ("the Great Garden," in Arabic), the summer retreat of the Moorish kings.

Inside the blank, red walls of the Alhambra are a series of gardens with courts surrounded by chambers and halls, but all at an intimate scale compared to the vastness of so much of Islamic architecture. There are pools and fountains fed through ancient aqueducts from the melting snows of the distant Sierras, and the shade of arcades and of cypresses. After centuries in the desert nothing was more desired by the Arabs than water and shade. The Court of the Myrtles, constructed for Yusuf I before 1350, has a long basin inhabited by large goldfish. The pool reflects the fortified tower above, and is flanked by masses of the fragrant evergreen shrub that gives the court its name.

Nearby is the Court of the Lions, built by Mohammed V during the second half of the fourteenth century, and the favorite haunt of Washington Irving, the famous author of *The Sketch Book,* who became United States Minister to Spain in 1842. His writings on Spanish history, and especially about the Alhambra, not only brought it fame but also did much to inspire its preservation by the Spanish government as a significant monument to Arab civilization as well as to a heroic period of the nation's historic past. "Here the hand of time has fallen the lightest," Irving wrote, "and the traces of Moorish elegance and splendour exist in almost their original brilliancy. Earthquakes have shaken the foundations of this pile, and rent its rudest

The Giralda, 12th century with 16th-century additions, Seville, Spain

towers, yet see—not one of these slender columns has been displaced, not an arch of that light and fragile colonnade has given way, and all the fairy fretwork of these domes, apparently as unsubstantial as the crystal fabrics of a morning's frost, yet exist after the lapse of centuries, almost as fresh as if from the hand of the Moslem artist."

In the center is a fountain whose basin is intricately carved in an interlaced design in relief, in-

The Alhambra, 13th–15th centuries, Granada, Spain

cluding a poetic inscription in praise of Allah for the blessing of water. Beneath it stand twelve stone lions spouting into a channel in the marble pavement that encircles the fountain. This feeds four other channels that extend at right angles, conducting the water into the rooms surrounding the court. At either end are airy pavilions with slender paired columns like those of the arcade that defines the court. Above the arches the wall is sculptured in a filigree pattern as fine as lace. The vaulting of the adjoining rooms is as fine in detail. Touched with blue and gold, it rises in a multiplication of tiny cells like those of a beehive, yet gives a curious cavelike effect because their pendant edges resemble stalactites. Passage from room to room is through strangely shaped arches whose profiles are serrated with the same pendant motive. Walls are diapered in repetitive lacy patterns in blue and green, surrounded by sinuous calligraphic inscriptions in delicate relief. There are vistas of alternating light and shade, with occasionally a breathtaking glimpse out of arched windows over the city far below. There is water flowing everywhere, in channels in the marble pavement, in basins, pools, and jets to cool the air, and in conduits beneath, so that there is a constant sound of murmuring and soft splashing.

From the Alhambra the Arab kings rode on horseback along a walled roadway up to the Generalife. Heavy gates were opened into a court where they dismounted, and then entered another court, surrounded by arches. These form a part of the Summer Palace, with its lookout towers and covered walks beside a long terrace planted with orange trees and myrtles "so thick and even," according to a description dating from just after the Reconquest, that from the upper gallery "they have the appearance of a dense lawn rather than the tops of trees . . . , and innumerable rabbits can be seen feeding and

The Court of the Myrtles, before 1350, The Alhambra

playing among the roots." Here, even more than in the Alhambra, water provided life and animation. There were no sculptures as in European gardens, and few flowering plants, only the blossoms of orange, oleander, and rose. But there were foliage and water everywhere, with tall jets framing a green vista of dark cypresses, in pools reflecting orange and lemon trees, and in canals bordered by rosebushes. Another terrace was "entirely covered with greenery; . . . by shutting off some of the channels without the person on the lawn being aware of it, the water is made to rise, . . . bursting through the lawn in countless fine sprays, bathing the occupant's feet and cooling him in the summer heat."

The gardens mount the hillside, terrace above

terrace, joined by fantastic stairs down whose hollowed balustrade cascades of water flow musically and collect in pools at every landing. Through groves of figs and oleanders one can climb to the very top, where from a tower there is a panorama miles in extent. One can look out over the gardens, the Alhambra, and westward down the channel of the Genil, whose waters make fertile the broad valley of the Vega. The city lies far below, dominated by the towering mass of the cathedral containing the tombs of Ferdinand of Aragon and Isabella of Castile, whose marriage united Spain and whose reign saw the discovery of the New World and the end of Arab dominion in the West. To the north, across the steep valley of the Darro,

mountain stronghold of the Arab kingdom of Granada. Thus they have both poetic unreality and a fantasy touched with melancholy that have fascinated people from the time they were constructed. Like the haunting Arab music one still hears there, they remain as a memory of Moorish splendor from a remote past, and as colorful and picturesque examples of the Oriental style that left such a significant impress on the art and culture of Spain.

Interior of The Alhambra

The Court of the Lions, after 1350, The Alhambra

is the hill called Sacromonte, its heights crowned by a monastery whose walls and towers gleam white in the brilliant southern sun.

The Alhambra and the Generalife have none of the triumphant scale and monumental grandeur of the great mosques of the Moslem empire. Sophisticated and fanciful, they represent the final expression of Arab art in the West. They were built as retreats from the realities of a shrinking world, as a last oasis of peace in the beleaguered

The Generalife, 12th–15th centuries, Granada, Spain

V   CHARLEMAGNE
AND THE EMPIRE OF THE WEST

On Christmas Day in the year 800, the great basilica of St. Peter in Rome was crowded to the doors with brightly robed cardinals and bishops, with monks and laymen, nobles and commoners, and with pilgrims from distant places. During the celebration of the Mass, amid the chanting of priests and choristers, Pope Leo III placed the heavy crown of the Holy Roman Empire upon the head of the most important visitor that Rome had seen in many a year as he knelt before the shrine of St. Peter. Leo then fell on his knees and did homage to the flaxen-haired giant who had united the German tribe of the Franks into a great kingdom, Charles, known to history as Charlemagne, Charles the Great. The coronation was an acknowledgment of Charles's preeminent position as leader in the West and the champion of the church.

The grandson of that other Charles, called the Hammer, who had vanquished the Moslems near Tour on the Loire sixty-eight years before, Charlemagne had spread Christianity by the sword among the Saxons to the north. He finally converted them from the worship of horse skulls nailed to the trees of sacred groves, a relic of their remote ancestry in the great plains far to the east. He had driven the Saracens south from the Pyrenees and established a Christian march north of the Ebro. Far to the east he had forced the proud Khan of the fierce Avars to accept Christianity along with his horde of Asiatic warriors, and he had defeated the Lombards and assumed the crown of the kingdom of Italy and the style of Patrician of Rome. His empire stretched from the Baltic to the Adriatic, and from the middle reaches of the Danube to northern Spain. His capital was at Aachen, or Aix-la-Chapelle, in the fertile Rhineland.

The Cathedral of St. Peter reechoed with shouts

Great Gold Brooch from the Sutton Hoo Treasure, Anglo-Saxon, 7th century. The British Museum, London

as all acclaimed the tall Frank as Carolus Augustus, Emperor of the Romans, heir of the Caesars, Protector of the Faith. Charlemagne himself did not relish the ceremony, which, according to his contemporary biographer, took him by surprise, because of its implications of papal supremacy—and this after the king himself had just restored Leo to his throne, liberating him from the dungeons of the family of his predecessor who had a mind to make the papacy hereditary and were therefore backing another candidate. Relations between Rome and Constantinople had been severed. The Empress Irene, having driven her son, the emperor, insane by torture and imprisonment, then blinded him, and ruled with a mad despotism that was doomed to destruction. Leo needed the support of the strongest man in Europe in such troubled times. The coronation was a formal recognition of the fact of Charlemagne's achievement. He had united the West under his political rule, and confirmed the Pope's leadership of the Latin Church with Rome as its center.

For more than three centuries there had been a restless movement of nomadic tribes from the north southward, and from the eastern plains westward as populations grew and one tribe clashed with another in the struggle for grazing lands for the flocks and herds that were their wealth. As they broke through the frontiers of the Roman Empire

Eagle Brooches, gilt bronze with garnets and other stones, almost 6″ high, Visigothic, 6th century. The Walters Art Gallery, Baltimore

in straggling hordes, burning, pillaging, and killing, the old order was destroyed. Strange gods were worshiped in even stranger ceremonies, with human sacrifice and ritual cannibalism. Pugnacious, impulsive, and illiterate, the tribesmen, whether the predominant Germans who settled the greater part of Europe, or Slavs, Iranians, or Mongols, brought with them also fierce individual-

Oseberg Monster, ca. 825, wood, about 5″ high. University Museum of Antiquities, Oslo, Norway

ism and a system of tribal loyalties that prevented organized effort or government.

They also brought a strange art that had had its

Carved Doorway from the Church at Urnes, Norway, ca. 1050

nature of the medieval world. In the meantime, however, there were two regions in the West, beyond the boundaries of the Empire, where barbarian art developed without crippling conflict to a dramatic climax. One was Scandinavia, where the pagans long resisted Christianity and clung to the old ways. The other was in the British Isles, and in Ireland, which had embraced Christianity earlier than many parts of northern Europe, and in northern England. There barbarian art became the means of expressing Christian faith with a passion and vigor that have almost never been equaled.

It was the custom in pagan times to bury Norse kings in their long boats, with their weapons and treasure around them, beneath great barrows of earth such as may still be seen in the British Isles, Scandinavia, Denmark, and Brittany. Occasionally archaeologists come upon one of these burials

Gallerus Oratory, County Kerry, Ireland

origins in the endless plains of Asia remote centuries before. It was a barbarous art, showing a taste for bright color and gleaming surface, and expressing its tremendous vitality in the use of dynamically curving linear forms. These were originally based on the animals that they hunted and that had become tribal totems, symbols of the supernatural and overwhelming powers of nature. It was emotional and irrational as befitted a people that acted from impulse and often with wild extravagance. It tended constantly toward the abstract, toward expression in line and form and color, rather than through the naturalistic representation of the human figure, as in the arts of Greece and Rome. As in the case of almost all nomadic peoples, it was also an art expressed mainly in small objects, in brooches, in jewelry, and in other adornment such as horse trappings and decorations for arms and armor.

When the barbarians were converted to Christianity, their traditional culture came into conflict with that derived from the Classic past, to the detriment of both. Eventually a powerful synthesis emerged in the eleventh century in the period called the Romanesque, because its architecture employed the massive masonry and the round arch of Rome. It also embodied certain forms and patterns of life derived from the Roman past, though dramatically transformed by the utterly different

which was not pillaged in ancient times, as at Oseberg in southern Norway. There excavation revealed among many other things a snarling monster that was a minor part of a Viking long boat of the early ninth century. The underlying form, based on knowing observation of animal life, is sufficiently convincing so that the abstract surface pattern of interlacing bands enhances its power. Like the dragon figureheads, it suggests something of the ferocity of the Viking raiders that was so compellingly expressed in that fervent prayer, said for centuries by all who lived near north Atlantic shores, "From the fury of the Norsemen, good Lord deliver us." The same designs appear on sword hilts, buckles, daggers, and jewelry, and after monks from Ireland and England brought Christianity to the northernmost regions in the tenth and eleventh centuries, on doors and portals of wooden churches, and on crosses and reliquaries. Barbarian art in Scandinavia long retained its intense vigor, but never rose to the heights of subtlety and expression of the art of Ireland and northern England.

Christianity had reached Britain while it was still a Roman province, and in the mid-fifth century St. Patrick led a group of missionaries from Gaul into Ireland. Ireland became a Christian refuge for many fleeing from Britain at the time of the invasions of the pagan Angles and Saxons, who proceeded to destroy whatever remnants of civilization remained from Roman times. Roman influence in Ireland, on the other hand, had been slight. It was a country of shepherds, farmers, and fishermen. And monasticism, with its ideal of a life dedicated to God and the service of God, flourished there in the original form that had developed in the Egyptian desert during the early years of the Christian era, when people sought to escape from persecution and to devote themselves to solitary meditation and prayer. Sometimes they lived in small communities, each with a separate hut or cell, and sometimes in the solitude of a remote place, feeling themselves closer there to the eternal things they sought. A few small buildings, like the Gallerus Oratory, remain as examples of the beehive construction in stone typical of the early monasteries.

The Irish monks were an independent lot, and found a rewarding way of life in monasticism of this pattern. Like most of Ireland's inhabitants, they were descended from Celtic tribesmen who had settled there hundreds of years before. Their church had been cut off from Rome for centuries after the abandonment of the province of Britain to the heathen conquerors. Celtic Christianity had developed independently and with none of the elaborate organization that the Church of Rome had taken over from the civil administration of the Empire. Monks were the teachers of Ireland, the devoted friends of the people, and the councilors of kings. Monasteries were centers of learning and the arts, and their scriptoria, or writing workshops, produced many Gospel and other books, each inscribed and illuminated with the care and beauty appropriate to its sacred message.

In the early spring of 563 a monk of an Irish princely family, later known as St. Columba, sailed from Ireland with twelve companions. They landed on the Isle of Saints, the tiny island of Iona off the west coast of Scotland, which for two hundred years thereafter was the vital center of Celtic Christianity. From there monks went out to convert the Scots and the Northumbrians, and to establish Celtic monasteries throughout the Continent.

Alarmed by the vigorous missionary activity of the Irish as it threatened his control of the church, in 596 Pope Gregory the Great sent out a prior named Augustine to reclaim southern Britain from the heathens. With the help of the Christian wife of the pagan king of Kent, Augustine established the see of Canterbury, of which he became the first archbishop, which has remained the religious capital of England ever since. Augustine was, like the Pope, a monk of the order founded a half century earlier at Monte Cassino in Italy by Benedict of Nursia. As a young man Benedict had been a

Iona: The Restored Cathedral and Monastic Buildings

Cross of Muireadach, *Monasterboice, County Louth, Ireland, 7th–9th centuries, stone monolith, 17' 8" high*

hermit, but he came to believe that the ideal holy life was to be lived with others according to what has ever since been known as the Rule of St. Benedict. The monks worked together during days regulated by prayers and services, under the direction of an abbot of their own election. The Rule was so practical and complete that it remains the basis of all such establishments down to our own day. It had the advantage for Gregory that since all monasteries were under his direct control, the monks became a highly organized and disciplined army to carry out the policies and purposes of the papacy.

In the contest between Rome and Ireland that was bound to follow, the superior force of Rome prevailed, but for more than two centuries there was a flowering of Irish Christianity whose effects were felt not only in the British Isles but in Europe from the Baltic to Italy. The church was enriched by the evangelical faith, the dedicated scholarship, and the strange and passionate art of the Irish monks. And after Charlemagne had won his empire, men trained in Celtic monasteries were among the cultural and religious leaders of a Europe emerging from the shadows of centuries of strife and barbarism.

Though there are a few early churches, dating from the seventh century on, in Kent and Northumbria in England, little is left of the ecclesiastical buildings constructed in Ireland during the early Middle Ages. What marauding Norsemen did not destroy, time and neglect have, and all that remains is a few ruins in remote places. But there are illuminated manuscripts, metalwork, and sculptured stone crosses that have come down to us as evidence of the extraordinary qualities of Celtic Christian art.

A number of the high crosses, variously dated from the seventh to the ninth century, are found on Iona, in the border country between England and Scotland, and in Ireland itself. Perhaps the most monumental of them is the one in the little Irish village of Monasterboice. It has the distinctive form peculiar to Celtic crosses, with the cross, the symbol of Christ's sacrifice, within the circle, a symbol of the "Sun of Creation" and of the universe. Through these forms the unknown Celtic sculptor expressed his belief in Christ's dominion as timeless and universal. The top of the cross takes the form of a reliquary called a house shrine because of its pitched roof decorated with a design suggesting shingles or slates. The entire surface of the cross is covered with panels in low relief cut

The Ardagh Chalice, *8th–9th centuries, goldsmith work with enamel, amber, glass, and crystal, 7" high. National Museum, Dublin*

St. Patrick's Bell Shrine, *ca. 1100, goldsmith work, about 9" high. National Museum, Dublin*

House Shrine, *Anglo-Irish, 8th century. Courtesy, Museum of Fine Arts, Boston. Theodora Wilbour Fund in Memory of Charlotte Beebe Wilbour*

into the fine-grained granitic stone. The crucifixion is the central subject, but there are many others: Adam and Eve, the Fall of Man, and further episodes, several of which are so exclusively Celtic in interpretation that their meaning is no longer clear. All form a complex whole whose purpose is to show the crucifixion in its religious context as the hope for salvation for all mankind. The unique form of these crosses, the obdurate hardness of the great slabs of stone from which they are made, and the density of the design, with each panel filled with its subject, the figures reduced to symbolic simplicity, make them impressive and moving witnesses to the faith inspired by Celtic missionaries from St. Columba's island monastery, so remote in both time and place that it seems to have belonged to another, and possibly a fresher and more hopeful, world.

The Ardagh Chalice, perhaps as early as the eighth century, is an example of the almost unbelievable intricacy of Irish goldsmith work. Made of three hundred and fifty-four separate pieces, it is a marvel of filigree in gold, silver, and bronze with enamel, amber, and glass. A microscope is needed to discover the fineness of its detail. Typical of the amazing completeness of the work and dedication of the artist is the fact that one of the most beautiful parts is hidden from sight on all occasions except when the chalice is emptied at the end of the Mass, because it is contained in the hollow bottom of the foot. There the unknown Irish craftsman set a crystal in a complex frame of amber, silver, and gold. The lip of the cup has the names of the twelve apostles delicately incised to form a decorative but meaningful border. As is the case with so many works of art of this remote time and place, nothing is known of where it was made or of who made it, but somehow it survived the dangers of time and Scandinavian raiders.

The Irish made bell shrines, cases of bronze, silver, and gold, elaborately decorated with goldsmith work, enamels, and precious stones. These were to contain the bell used by some early churchman to call together his flock for worship beneath some tall stone cross. Through association with his saintly memory the shrine took on the aura of a sacred relic. There were house shrines, caskets

for relics in a shape like that of the top of the Cross of Monasterboice. Such shrines came down in certain families whose members acted as hereditary keepers through centuries of time. There were book shrines also, since nothing was more highly valued than illuminated manuscripts. As Irish scribes lavished lifetimes of care and artistry on them, they created the model of the medieval book. Their works were sought by pope and emperor, and became the treasures of monastic libraries throughout Europe.

The most remarkable of them, considered by many as one of the most beautiful manuscripts in the world, is the Book of Kells. It is a Gospel book

St. John, Book of Kells, *late 8th century. Trinity College, Dublin*

St. Matthew, Book of Kells, *late 8th century. Trinity College, Dublin*

Initial Page for the Gospel of St. John, Book of Kells, late 8th century. Trinity College, Dublin

Interior of the Palace Chapel of Charlemagne at Aachen, 792–805

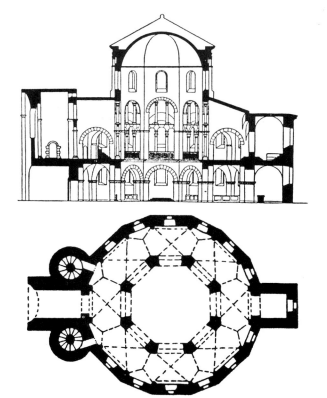

Restored Plan and Section of the Palace Chapel of Charlemagne at Aachen

that was probably made in St. Columba's abbey of Iona at the end of the eighth century, and taken to Ireland after the destruction of the abbey by Norsemen, when the monks of Iona refounded the monastery of Kells in 802, just two years after the coronation of Charlemagne in distant Rome. As was the custom in Irish manuscripts, each of the four Gospels has a page devoted to the portrait of the Evangelist whose name it bears, then an initial page followed by the text of the Gospel.

In colors of pale yellow, blue, soft red, green, and violet, the Irish scribe transformed the familiar classical portraits of Matthew, Mark, Luke, and John into abstract patterns of immense subtlety and power. The initial pages overflow with luxuriant invention. Human, animal, and plant forms are integrated into a unique system of abstract linear design that surges and intertwines in constant movements, yet remains under constant control. The eye can hardly trace the complexities of the interlace in any given area. The effect of the whole is one of bursting vitality. A dynamic energy sings through the pages with passionate and mystical faith. The book is as vividly alive today as when, more than twelve hundred years ago, an unknown monk, after years of dedicated work in a tiny beehive cell of stones on a distant island, alone with the sound of the sea, the wind, and the cries of gulls, finally completed the greatest masterpiece of Celtic art.

Like Constantine, Charlemagne had a sacred palace at his capital at Aachen in the Rhineland, but it was called the Lateran, because there was a tradition that the church had given the Lateran in Rome to Constantine for an imperial residence. Inside the entrance of Charlemagne's palace chapel was the Roman she-wolf in bronze, brought from Italy. The chapel itself was patterned as nearly after the imperial Church of S. Vitale in Ravenna as his architects could make it. The result, however, has none of the soaring lightness of the earlier church. Instead, the chapel is stocky and somber. The westwork, a completely northern development of the vestibule and facade into an architectural unit heavily emphasized with a massive tower, has nothing to do with either the Eastern or the classical traditions, though it was to become a feature of German church architecture for centuries. The chapel's blunt, golden dome rose above the complex of lower buildings lying in a landscape with thick groves of trees, and herds of grazing deer. An equestrian statue of Theodoric, greatest of the earlier German rulers, was imported from Ravenna to stand in the great court of the palace, and there was a tremendous swimming pool where, according to contemporary report, the Emperor and a hundred companions could bathe at once.

The palace was thronged with people — soldiers and clerics, merchants and nobles, envoys from Rome and Constantinople, Gothic and Slavic chieftains with their barbarous retinues, turbaned Moslems from Africa and Spain. There was even an ambassador from the great Harun al-Rashid, Caliph of Baghdad, and the most powerful ruler in the Islamic world, master of a far richer and more sophisticated capital than that of the Frankish Emperor to whom he sent the wondrous gift of an elephant. Court costumes were colorful, with more than a little flavor of barbaric taste, though the silks for ceremonial robes and vestments came from the East. From there also came the Asiatic spices used liberally at the table, in days before refrigeration, to disguise the taste of meats served in massive gold dishes, and to flavor the

Ivory Book Cover of the Gospels of Lorsch, *early 9th century. Vatican Library, Rome*

wines drunk from jeweled goblets. The vast imperial estates produced food enough to feed the crowds of people that came and went, including the scores of officers that kept contact with the imperial armies, whether they were in the field on some distant frontier or in winter camp.

Charlemagne himself traveled constantly, and whenever he could, tirelessly discussed politics, science, religion, and philosophy with the many distinguished persons who were attracted to his court from all parts of the world. He invited the great scholar Alcuin of York, from Northumbria in England, to help establish schools for the education of both clerics and laymen so that they could become more effective administrators for governing the Empire. The Emperor himself studied with Alcuin, and slept with a book beneath his pillow for wakeful moments. The imperial school system demanded texts, and the many new churches and monasteries needed Gospels, Psalters, and other books. Scribes working at the court and in the many monastic centers throughout the Empire,

Ivory Book Cover of the Gospels of Lorsch, *early 9th century. Victoria and Albert Museum, London*

figures on ivories made in Constantinople, like that of the Archangel Michael of the early sixth century. One cover shows Christ standing between angels and treading underfoot the beasts, symbols of evil, described in the Ninety-first Psalm. As in the statue of the Good Shepherd and the mosaic in the tomb of Galla Placidia, Christ is young and beardless according to the Classic tradition. Above, two angels hold a medallion with the cross. Below, the Magi appear before Herod, to the left, and to the right, present their gifts to the Christ-child. On the other cover the Virgin and Child are enthroned between saints, angels hold a medallion of Christ blessing, above, and below, are the Nativity and the Annunciation to the Shepherds. Despite the tiny scale, these narrative scenes have complete clarity. The carving has an amazing fineness and sensitivity, and the pattern of the curving folds of drapery and of architectural detail animates the whole design. Yet the faces have complete repose, and their large eyes stare past us with Byzantine detachment into another world.

The manuscript itself has a similar sober dignity. On one page, brilliant with gold against red, blue, and yellow, a youthful Christ sits enthroned, His hand raised in blessing, within a circular glory inscribed with the symbols of the four Evangelists.

in what are today France, Germany, Switzerland, Spain, and Italy, produced manuscripts written in the clear and readable Carolingian script that is the basis of all our printing today. Many are richly illuminated with miniatures in reds, blues, greens, and gold. A few of the most sumptuous, perhaps those destined for the library of the Emperor or his friends, had pages dyed in the rare and costly purple of Tyre. Other craftsmen added their skills to those of the scribe, for many of the books were bound in covers made by goldsmiths and set with enameled plaques and precious stones, and sometimes panels of carved ivory.

One of the most beautiful of Carolingian books is the ivory-covered manuscript called the Gospels of Lorsch from the name of a monastery on the Rhine where it was kept for many years. Like many manuscripts, it was later divided, so that today the text and one cover are in the Vatican in Rome and the other cover is in the Victoria and Albert Museum in London. The carved covers strongly resemble the aloof and delicately cut

St. John, Gospels of Lorsch, *early 9th century. Vatican Library, Rome*

Above and below are inscriptions in capital letters that are as clear and well formed as if taken from a monument of imperial Rome. At the beginning of each Gospel is a portrait of the Evangelist, seated beneath his symbol. Curtains are drawn aside to reveal St. John as a serious young man holding an open book in his left hand while dipping a pen into a tiny inkwell with his right.

The most remarkable manuscript of Carolingian times is that known as the Utrecht Psalter because it has been in the possession of the library of that famous Netherlandish university since the eighteenth century. About the year 830 its 108 vellum pages, containing the psalms and the sacred songs of the Old Testament, were illustrated by an unknown artist in a series of drawings unique in the world. Each psalm has an illustration, and just as one figure of speech tumbles after another in the psalmist's verses, the illustrator's swift pen rushes to express a dynamic visualization of each of them. His interpretation is entirely literal. For the line "Awake, why sleepest thou, O Lord?" he shows the Lord asleep in bed with angels trying vainly to awaken Him. For "Now will I arise, saith the Lord," he draws Him springing to His feet from the globe of the world that serves as His throne throughout the Psalter, and leaping forward out of the oval glory that surrounds His figure in answer to the psalmist's prayer for aid.

There is no color except for the red of initials, and there is no formal design. Both the coherence and the extraordinary effectiveness of the work

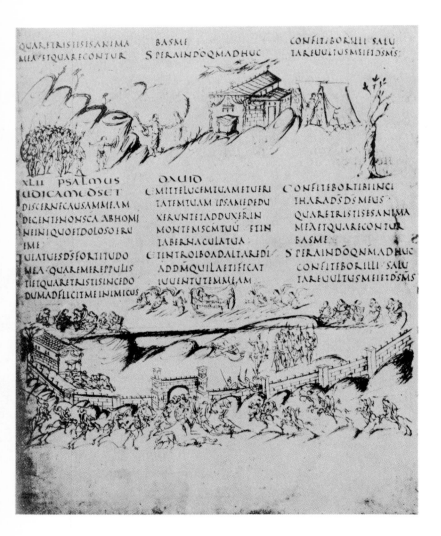

Psalm 12, from the Utrecht Psalter, *ca. 820. University Library, Utrecht, The Netherlands*

Psalm 43, from the Utrecht Psalter, *ca. 820. University Library, Utrecht, The Netherlands*

are the result of the artist's curious headlong style. His line seems charged with electricity. The tiny figures are vibrant with nervous energy. They gesture, flee, supplicate, charge madly, and grapple in desperate combat, or wait tensely in momentary stillness. The landscape undulates, the hand of God thrusts downward through the clouds. Angels' wings and draperies flutter. The unknown artist's curious and compelling style is a translation into graphic illustration of the vitality of the barbaric tradition. It is instinct with the same energy that informs the Celtic interlace of the Book of Kells.

There was much coming and going throughout the Empire and beyond during Charlemagne's reign. Because such small objects as manuscripts, ivory carvings, and metalwork were not only portable but highly valued, they were taken from place to place and often presented as gifts. As a result they were transmitters of both styles and concepts, and became models not only for similar objects but also for painting and sculpture on a large scale. Apses of churches were frescoed according to designs borrowed from manuscripts or enamels, and church portals sculptured in schemes derived from carved ivories. In this way, from the time of Charlemagne on, the two major trends running through the arts of the earlier Middle Ages were spread far and wide. For centuries thereafter we can see the combination and alternation of the repose and restraint of the Classic tradition, as seen in the Lorsch Gospels, with the expressive linear vitality of the Utrecht Psalter, the heritage of the tribal art of the barbarians.

Charlemagne's amazing energy appeared in everything he did, and his powerful personality dominated his era. He arranged for his own tomb in the palace church, a great stone sarcophagus with the inscription that "beneath this stone lies the Body of Charles the Great ... Orthodox Emperor ..." When, on a bitter day late in January, 814, he died at seventy-one in his palace at Aachen, there was no one to maintain the colossal inheritance that he left. Without his personality and force to unite it, the far-flung elements of his Empire broke up into fragments from which gradually evolved the present states of Europe.

Sixty-seven years after Charlemagne's death, Viking raiders destroyed the life-size statue above his tomb with furious battle-axes as they ravaged the disintegrating Empire, and shadows again gathered across Europe. But his reign provided later ages with an epic tradition that rivaled that of the ancient heroes of Homeric Greece, as the

Carving from the Prow of The Oseberg Ship, ca. 825. University Museum of Antiquities, Oslo, Norway

deeds of the Emperor and his paladins against the Saracens were sung by minstrels in castle halls for centuries to come. Further, it again lent hope to the old ideal of a great peaceful empire stretching from the misty isles of Britain to the Holy Land, an ideal of a united world that is still the dream of men today.

VI PILGRIMS AND CRUSADERS

Lost in a narrow valley in the wooded hills of Aquitaine in southern France lies the tiny village of Conques. A handful of ancient houses cling to the steep slopes above the swift-flowing little river Louche. They cluster about the stone bulk of the Church of Ste.-Foy, whose three slate-covered towers dominate the town. Chickens peck among the cobbles of the narrow, winding streets, undisturbed by the passing of villagers, or a herd of goats or an occasional cow being driven to pasture with the help of a knowing dog. The village seems to sleep and dream of the past when it was a major stopping place on one of the most traveled roads in history, the Road of St. James, leading to the

Conques, with the Church of Ste.-Foy, France

cathedral dedicated to that apostle at Santiago de Compostela in northwest Spain.

Though Ste.-Foy is not an extraordinarily large church, it has a sober dignity in the almost undecorated simplicity of its exterior, in the austere surfaces of its stone walls, and in the surprising loftiness of its nave. It is a dignity befitting its importance as the shrine of the girl saint, martyred during the persecution of Diocletian, the predecessor of Constantine the Great. Her relics are reported to have performed so many miracles that her fame spread throughout the Christian World. Her church at Conques was sought by pilgrims from far and near.

The eleventh century saw the start of the age of pilgrimages, when, in a search for salvation, people took to the roads to worship at the shrines of saints. Some went barefoot and some were shod, while others rode horses or donkeys. Some approached the holy places they sought on their knees, while others measured their length upon the ground. A pilgrimage could be as short as to the next county, or it could mean a dangerous trip of thousands of miles, taking many months or even years. Increasingly, three objectives came to outweigh all others: Rome the eternal city and home of the Church; the Holy Land, where Christianity was born; and the shrine of Santiago, or St. James, at Compostela. Hostile strangers often barred the way to Jerusalem, though for some centuries tolerant Moslem rulers were quite willing to have Christians enter their territories provided they came in peace. But fellow Christians often proved as dangerous as the infidel in some of the sparsely inhabited country through which the pilgrims had to pass. So hostels were built along the way, usually in connection with an important church or monastery, or at particularly dangerous places, such as that of St. Bernard, whose monks, with the help of their famous dogs, saved countless lives of travelers caught in the treacherous snows of the Alpine pass.

Many hostels were founded by the Benedictine monks of the powerful order of Cluny, which established monasteries throughout the south of France and in Spain, modeled after its motherhouse in Burgundy. The Third Church at Cluny, begun by its greatest abbot, St. Hugh, in about 1088, was larger than Old St. Peter's in Rome, and dominated the immense monastic fortress, with its fifteen towers rising high above its circuit of walls. A five-aisled basilica, it could hold the multitude of people who thronged to join in the impressive celebrations of the major feast days. It served as a prototype for many churches, and was the greatest of a group built at Tours, Toulouse, Limoges, and elsewhere along the Pilgrimage Road, including

Cluny Abbey, as of 1798, when the demolition began. Restoration study made under the auspices of the Mediaeval Academy of America by K. J. Conant. Surroundings, a modern air view by Combier, Mâcon. Published by arrangement with the author

St. James itself. Monks of Cluny became popes and bishops, and sculptors employed in adorning its church were among the leading artists of their age. Until Cluny was finally destroyed early in the nineteenth century, its church remained one of the greatest in Christendom and an important place of pilgrimage in its own right.

Cluny Abbey, Interior of the Third Church. Restoration study made under the auspices of the Mediaeval Academy of America by K. J. Conant, assisted by T. C. Bannister. Published by arrangement with the author

Church of St.-Sernin, ca. 1080–1120, Toulouse, France

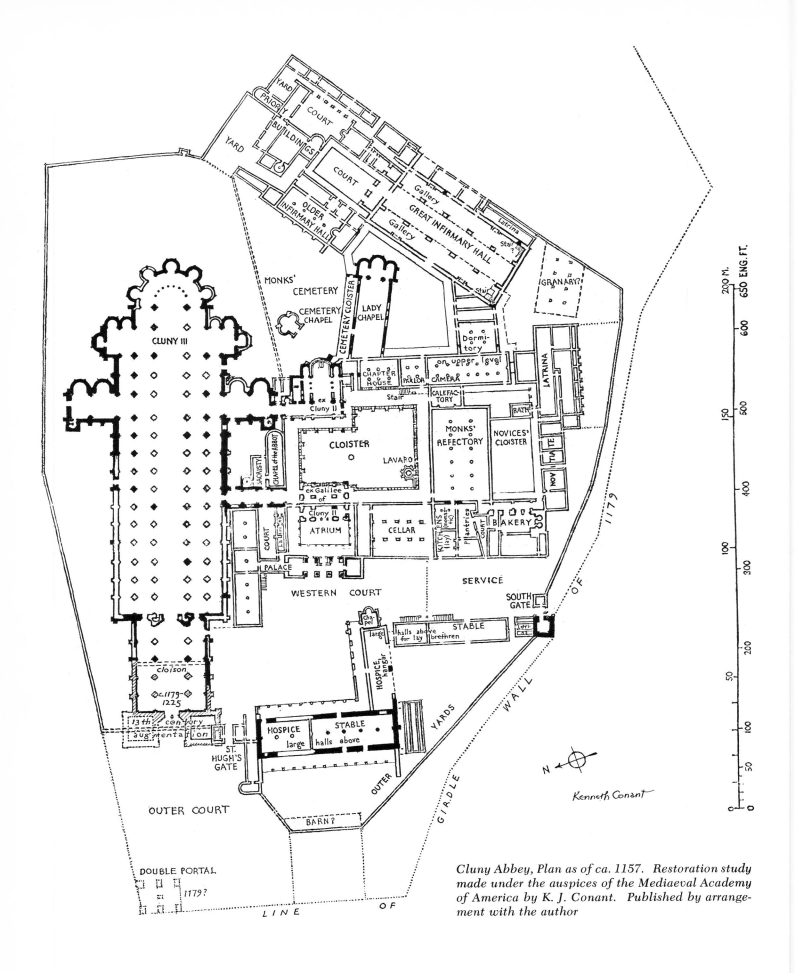

YARD

PRIORY
BUILDINGS
COURT

YARD

COURT

OLDER
INFIRMARY HALL

Gallery

Gallery

GREAT INFIRMARY HALL

Latrina
stair

GRANARY?

MONKS'
CEMETERY

CEMETERY CLOISTER

CEMETERY
CHAPEL

LADY
CHAPEL

CLUNY III

Dormi-
tory

on upper level

CHAPTER
HOUSE

PARLOR

CAMERA

LATRINA

ex
Cluny II

Stair

CALEFAC-
TORY

BATH

SACRISTY

CHAPEL of the ABBOT

CLOISTER

LAVABO

MONKS'
REFECTORY

NOVICES'
CLOISTER

NOVITIATE

ex Galilee
of

COURT

ex
Cluny II

ATRIUM

CELLAR

KITCHENS
(lay)

monks'

Pantries

COURT

BAKERY

PALACE

WESTERN COURT

SERVICE

cloison

c.1179-
1225

13th century
augmenta ion

ST.
HUGH'S
GATE

HOSPICE
large

STABLE
halls above

OUTER

YARDS

chapel

large

HOSPICE, hangar

halls above
for lay brethren

STABLE

SOUTH
GATE

latri
na

GIRDLE   WALL   OF   1179

N

Kenneth Conant

OUTER COURT

BARN?

DOUBLE PORTAL

1179?

LINE   OF

*Cluny Abbey, Plan as of ca. 1157. Restoration study
made under the auspices of the Mediaeval Academy
of America by K. J. Conant. Published by arrangement with the author*

200 M.

650 ENG. FT.

600

150

500

400

100

300

50

200

100

50

0   0

Cathedral of Santiago de Compostela. Restoration study of original scheme (ca. 1078) by K. J. Conant. Published by arrangement with the author

During the course of the eleventh century regular routes from different parts of Europe were established. Englishmen, like Chaucer's famous pilgrims, followed the line of the old Roman roads to Canterbury. From there they journeyed to a Channel port and by boat to France, trending westward toward Santiago, or eastward toward Rome, and perhaps from there even on to the yet more distant Holy Land. Other routes led from northern and eastern Europe and eventually joined, to cross either the Alps into Italy or the Pyrenees into Spain. No one knows how many people left their homes to go on pilgrimages during the Middle Ages, but there were thousands upon thousands of them, and perhaps the greater number went to Santiago. People even called the Milky Way "the Way of St. James," since it seemed reassuringly to guide their steps toward Compostela, whose very name means "field of stars," even after darkness had made a strange country seem stranger still.

In the twelfth century a pious cleric wrote a *Guide for the Pilgrim of Santiago*, which described the Road and the shrines on the way, such as the shrine of St. Martin, the Apostle of Gaul, at Tours, the greatest pilgrim center in France. The *Guide* told of the basilica of St.-Sernin at Toulouse, with its tall tower that could be seen from afar, and its reliefs of angels and prophets sculptured with Roman solidity and roundness of form. It told of the hostels at which one could stay, and the perils of the journey. It described the huge cross at the crest of a pass of the Pyrenees where Charlemagne himself had knelt to pray, his face turned toward Santiago, and where all the pilgrims followed his example. It pointed out the pass at Roncevaux, where the great paladin Roland, the Emperor's companion, had finally died a hero's death at the hand of the Moors. He had slain hundreds of them with a sword so terrible that it clove at a blow a stone that was still to be seen in front of the church that had been built there.

The Road crossed that famous battlefield and led on through the heights of Navarre, where the *Guide* warned pilgrims to beware of the Basques whom they would meet there. They were bare-legged mountain men, wearing short fringed coats and sandals of leather cured with the hair on it. They bore two spears apiece and a horn to summon others, though sometimes they hooted like owls or howled like wolves, and suddenly a pilgrim band might be surrounded by a menacing horde of them. In the lower country beyond, the wayfarers followed the old Roman road westward into Galicia through hills and valleys as green as Ireland.

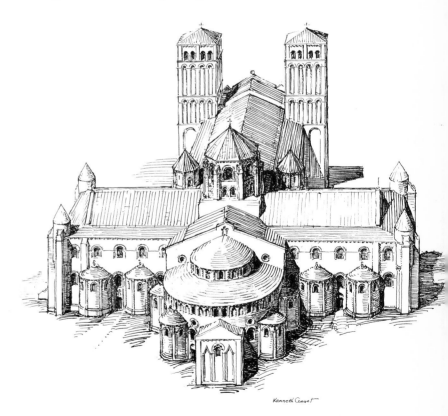

Cathedral of Santiago de Compostela. Restoration study of the west front as projected, and largely built, 1168–1211. Restoration study by K. J. Conant. Published by arrangement with the author

Finally, from the top of Monte San Marcos, if the day was clear, they could discern the distant towers of the basilica of St. James. The first to see it was acclaimed king of the pilgrims by the others, an honor that was passed down with pride from generation to generation. At last, after months of danger and hardship, they could kneel at the tomb of the apostle saint who was believed to have brought Christianity to Spain, and inspired the crusade against the Moors.

The great church of Santiago was almost identical in plan and appearance, though not in size, to the Churches of St.-Sernin in Toulouse and Ste.-Foy in Conques, because there were architects and sculptors among those who traveled the Pilgrimage Road. Ideas and special skills went along with the pilgrims, as well as stories of saints and legends of the lands through which they passed, the epic deeds of Charlemagne and his paladins, and of Arthur and the Knights of the Round Table. Songs went with the pilgrims too, some of them popular hymns full of the faith and hope that inspired them. Others were gay and often humorous and bawdy to lighten the long days of tiresome travel and relieve the solitude of strange places.

The Pilgrimage Road was far from being any sort of highway that we would recognize as such today. In some places where it led from village to village, or as it approached a market town, it might have been passable for wagons. But in others it was just a track, hardly distinguishable from some local cow path. Across streams and rivers too deep to ford, there were ferries, or occasionally bridges, mostly left over from Roman times, often maintained by monks or groups of dedicated laymen. Bridge-building was considered an important act

of piety, and many bridges were constructed during the Middle Ages. Among the most famous were old London Bridge, designed by an engineer-monk named Peter of Colechurch in 1176, and the bridge across the Rhône, which tradition ascribes to the vision of a shepherd boy, later to be known as St. Bénézet, where every year boys and girls still dance in a circle, as in the words of the old song, "sur le pont d'Avignon."

Apse Frescoes from the Church of San Clemente de Tahull, Spain, ca. 1125. Museum of Catalonian Art, Barcelona

Churches and monasteries near the Road were accustomed to taking care of unexpected bands of pilgrims who often slept in the cloister when there was no shelter elsewhere. In each church or chapel the pilgrims prayed. Sometimes they knelt before such overpowering images of God as those which were painted by an unknown artist on the vault of the Church of San Clemente in the village of Tahull in western Catalonia, and now preserved in the Museum of Catalonian Art in Barcelona. Dating from shortly after 1123 when the church was dedicated, the frescoed figure of Christ as judge, in the curving shell of the apse, loomed overhead in the half-light of the dim interior. En-

Bridge of St. Bénézet, 12th century, Avignon, France

throned within a rainbowlike glory, Christ raises one hand in blessing, while the other holds a book inscribed *Ego Sum Lux Mundi* ("I am the light of the world"). The symbols of the four Evangelists surround Him, and His intense gaze seems directed at each person individually. The stylized folds of drapery and the limitless blue of heaven behind Him enhance the feeling of austere strength that became a major quality of Spanish medieval art. Above, the slender and immense hand of God reaches down through the clouds and appears thrust miraculously through the vault itself. Never have the familiar images and symbols received such a relentlessly powerful expression as in embattled Spain, where for centuries Christianity waged a war for survival, and churches and monasteries were often fortified outposts of the faith in a harsh land largely dominated by the infidel.

Wyvern, *from the Frescoes from San Pedro de Arlanza, Spain, ca. 1220. The Metropolitan Museum of Art, New York, The Cloisters Collection, Gift of John D. Rockefeller, Jr., 1931*

The Hand of God, *Detail from the Frescoes from the Church of San Clemente de Tahull*

Lion, *from the San Pedro de Arlanza Frescoes. The Metropolitan Museum of Art, New York, The Cloisters Collection, Gift of John D. Rockefeller, Jr., 1931*

The same fierceness of expression is conveyed by the winged dragon and the strutting lion with lashing tail, painted about 1220, that once guarded the monks at their meetings in the chapter house of the monastery of San Pedro de Arlanza near Burgos, and are now in The Cloisters in New York.

The motives for such immense designs traveled along the Road with the pilgrims. They were carried in the minds and memories of monks, in the sketchbooks of artisans, and in illuminated manuscripts such as one from the early thirteenth century now preserved in The Pierpont Morgan Library in New York. This famous book, a *Commentary on the Revelation of St. John*, was written in 784 in a monastery, hidden from the Arabs in a remote valley of the Asturian Mountains, by Beatus, Abbot of Liebana. His work was copied and recopied for centuries in many different manuscripts. All were illustrated with the strange, remote intensity that fired the imagination of the sculptor of the *Apostles Receiving the Holy Spirit* over the door of the Church of St. Mary Magdalene at Vézelay (1120–1132) in Burgundy. It inspired the passionate, ascetic saints and prophets that seem almost dancing their ecstatic adoration, carved at about the same time on the portals of the Church of St.-Pierre at Moissac, and a few years later, of the Abbey Church of Souillac, both farther south along the Road.

Illumination from a 13th-century Manuscript of the Commentary on the Revelation of St. John. *The Pierpont Morgan Library, New York*

Through the mountains the Road was steep and narrow, clinging to perilous slopes, and skirting dangerous gorges. Crosses or cairns of stones marked where some had died on the way, and tiny chapels, built by pious hands, provided rest and shelter in remote places. Increasingly the stations on the Road became important for religious as well

The Prophet Isaiah, *on the South Portal of the Church of St.-Pierre, Moissac, France, ca. 1115. Archives Photographiques—Paris*

as practical reasons, as the fame of their various saints spread. Thus the power of the girl martyr, Saint Foy, made Conques a place of miracles.

The Road to Conques and thence to Santiago wound southward from Burgundy for miles through the rough and heavily wooded heights of central France. The great bell of the monastery of the warrior monks of Aubrac tolled nightly to guide the steps of pilgrims, overtaken by darkness, through the steep uplands of the Cévennes. Finally they came down into the valley of the Louche and could see the towers of the Abbey of Ste.-Foy. They entered the town through the fortified gate and made their way to the tall church, where they drank from the spring that rises just in front of it, and paused devoutly to study the relief of the Last Judgment over the portal. In it the sculptor showed with graphic clarity the fate in store for the sinful who are being attacked and tortured by ingenious and tireless devils, while the saved stand serene and smiling at Christ's right hand. Then the pilgrims entered the church through the wide door beneath the famous carving. Inside, the nave

The Last Judgment, *Tympanum of the Church of Ste.-Foy, Conques, France, 12th century. Archives Photographiques—Paris*

rose to the plain barrel vault high above. Light from the lantern tower poured down into the crossing, and the march of the piers down the nave was continued by the columns around the east end that closed the long vista. But they saw little then of the quiet beauty of the church interior, because their entire attention was directed toward what they had come far to seek, the Golden Majesty of Conques, gleaming on the high altar.

The Prophet Isaiah, *on the Main Portal of the Abbey Church of Souillac, France, ca. 1110. Archives Photographiques—Paris*

Nave of the Church of Ste.-Foy, Conques, France. Archives Photographiques—Paris

The reliquary statue does not look like that of a young girl, but rather, like a queen who reigns serenely in the church as her holy palace. Entirely of gold, she sits on a golden throne that is ornamented with globes of clear crystal. Her robes and the throne alike are studded with precious stones, brilliant enamel plaques, and engraved gems from ancient Greece and Rome. Her crown is encrusted with cameos and jewels, and even her slippers, resting on a silk pillow, are rich with gold and gems. One forgets that the figure is really merely a reliquary, a container for a few fragments of the belt from the dress of a little girl who died bravely so long ago. The eleventh-century goldsmith has given the Golden Majesty a presence that can be felt. With eyes of brilliant blue enamel, she stares straight ahead in regal dignity, and holds forth in each hand, with a delicacy as entirely feminine as the elaborate earrings, two little vials of gold in which were placed tiny bouquets of flowers when the statue was carried in procession.

The Golden Majesty of Ste.-Foy did reign over the domain of the Abbey of Conques, and her influence went much farther afield. If there was an epidemic among the people or a blight on the crops, she was carried forth from her sanctuary to put things to rights. There were so many miracles ascribed to her that the monks could scarcely record them all. As garlands of iron fetters hung in the church as votive offerings gave witness, she delivered prisoners from captivity. She settled disputes between villages, and kept ambitious barons from seizing lands belonging to the abbey.

When the statue was taken on such a mission, it was carefully placed on a litter between two slow-pacing horses, and accompanied by a procession of chanting monks led by the abbot in full vestments. Young clerks clashed cymbals and blew blasts on ivory horns to warn of its coming, and everywhere it went, the abbey's chronicles tell us, the harmony of man and nature was restored. Once it was carried miles to the south toward Albi, whose people begged the blessing of the presence of the relics of the saint. It was mounted on a wagon drawn by white oxen, their horns bright with gold. At every village, people gathered at the sound of the cymbals and of the ivory horns. At night a canopy was raised over it, decorated with green boughs, just as had been the statues of the Great Mother, the earth goddess who had been worshiped there in pagan times so many centuries before.

Every church in that part of France aspired to have such a statue containing the relics of its patron saint. Though some statues were made of bronze, many were of silver, and others of gold. At the synod, or ecclesiastical council, of Rodez early in the eleventh century a number were brought from the churches of those clerics attending. They were placed in a meadow near the city gates, each on a platform, and sheltered under a bright canopy and exhibited to the wonderment and awe of all the people, who found them even more impressive than the bishops and other dignitaries of the church in all the finery of rich vestments. Most of these reliquary statues are gone now. Many were destroyed during the French Revolution, while others disappeared during other times of strife and violence. But the Golden Majesty still reigns in the Church of Ste.-Foy in the tiny village of Conques to remind us not only of the artistry but also of the faith of France of the eleventh century.

Of all the wandering barbarian tribes that played a part in the troubled history of the Middle Ages, none was more feared than the Vikings. They harried the coasts of Europe, rowed their dragon ships up the rivers and pillaged and plundered almost at will, so unexpected and swift was their attack, and so irresistible the force of their great swords and battle-axes. They established the first kingdom in Russia, formed the elite guard of the Byzantine Emperor, and sailed their long boats across the Atlantic to Iceland, Greenland, Labrador, and beyond.

The Golden Majesty of Ste.-Foy, *11th century Reliquary of goldsmith work with gems, precious and semiprecious stones, and enamels. Archives Photographiques — Paris*

east coast of the Adriatic from the Byzantine Empire, all with the pope's blessing.

It was William, the descendant of Rollo and the bastard son of Robert the Devil and the daughter of a tanner, who became a later Duke of Normandy and the conqueror of England. "Stark he was to men who withstood him," wrote a contemporary chronicler; "so harsh and cruel he was that none withstood his will." Violent, ruthless, and able, William launched his invasion in 1066, and on the day of the Archangel Michael, saint of battles, he defeated King Harald at Hastings and wiped out the Saxon opposition.

The story is told visually in the famous embroidery inaccurately called the Bayeux Tapestry, now in the Town Hall of that ancient Norman city. It was worked in colored wools on a 230-foot linen strip within a decade or two after the events it portrays so graphically. The embroidery shows Norman long boats, their gunwales lined with shields, and mounted knights armed with hauberk and helm, and ends in a furious battle scene with somersaulting horses and the death of Harald, fighting to the last. William divided the kingdom among his followers as Rollo had done. He made each man answerable to him personally for his fief, thus establishing the most complete feudal monarchy yet to appear in history. He replaced Saxon clergy with Normans. The administration of the country he left largely to his warrior half-brother, Odo, Bishop of Bayeux, who went into battle swordless but swinging a tremendous mace "so that," as a good churchman and Christian, "he might shed no blood."

The conquerors introduced the new fashion in architecture that had already begun to appear in Normandy. As symbols of Norman control of the subject population, tall, bare stone churches rose to replace the earlier, smaller, and more richly decorated Saxon buildings. In Durham, in the far north of England, Bishop William of St. Carileph tore down the Saxon Church of St. Cuthbert, famous for its beauty. As a part of a fortress against the marauding Scots, he began the construction of a new cathedral in August of the year 1093. The work went swiftly, since by 1133 the building was substantially complete. It was one of the largest medieval churches in Europe, with a nave one third wider than that of the great pilgrimage Church of St.-Sernin at Toulouse, and four hundred feet in length. It was revolutionary in its construction. Here for the first time appears the system of compartmented vaults, divided by arches crossing

In the year 911, however, Rollo, perhaps the most successful of the Norse pirates, who had ravaged England, the Low Countries, and much of France, established himself at Rouen and gave his oath of fealty to the King of the Franks. He was made Duke of the province thereafter to be known as Normandy, for thus the Norsemen became the Normans. Rollo divided the duchy among his leading warriors, governed his captured people strictly but well, and was converted into a devout and enthusiastic Christian. During the following century and a half the Normans conquered Southern Italy and Sicily from the Saracens, and much of the

Archbishop Odo of Bayeux Encourages the Normans to Attack the Saxon Army, *Detail from the* Bayeux Tapestry, *ca. 1073–1083, embroidered in wool on linen, 20″ high. Town Hall, Bayeux, France*

the nave at regular intervals, and each compartment set within a stone framework of groins, or diagonally crossing arches, so that the thrusts of the vaults are collected at the points where the groins meet above the piers. This allowed the stone filling of the compartments to be lighter and thinner than is possible with a barrel vault such as that at St.-Sernin. The massive round arches are a symbol of the Romanesque style. The toothed and zigzag designs of the moldings and the bold chevrons, diagonals, verticals, and diamond patterns of the immense round columns that alternate with clustered piers in the nave emphasize the masculine strength and austerity of the Norman ideal.

High on steep cliffs within a protecting loop of the river Wear, the bare bulk of the church rises to squat square towers flanking the heavy facade. The tall lantern above the crossing stands like a watchtower to guard the troubled border country. From this fortress-church the Prince-Bishops of Durham ruled the Palatinate with a stern Norman hand, riding forth with falcon at the wrist and a guard of armored knights and men-at-arms on tours of inspection. They led their troops into battle against fierce northern tribesmen who periodically swept down from Scotland to harry the farms and villages in the surrounding counties in the centuries of local and national conflict. The bravery and treachery of these forays were memorialized in the

The Cathedral of Durham from across the Wear

border ballads, so beloved of Sir Walter Scott, that continued to be sung in the remote parts of the countryside even into the beginning of our own century.

The age was one of violence throughout Europe. Not pope, nor emperor, nor king could control the unruly barons who constantly fought among themselves to add to their territories and power, or for the pure joy of combat and pillage. Out of the ancient barbarian tradition of personal allegiance of warrior to leader had developed the feudal system. Each man, theoretically at least, owed a personal allegiance to his overlord, who might be king, bishop, or noble. At the lord's demand, the vassal, as the follower was called, had to perform the feudal duty specified in the agreement by which he held his fief, or estate. It might be to take the field at the head of a specified number of knights and men-at-

The Death of King Harald, *Detail from the* Bayeux Tapestry

Interior of the Cathedral of Durham, England, 1093–1133

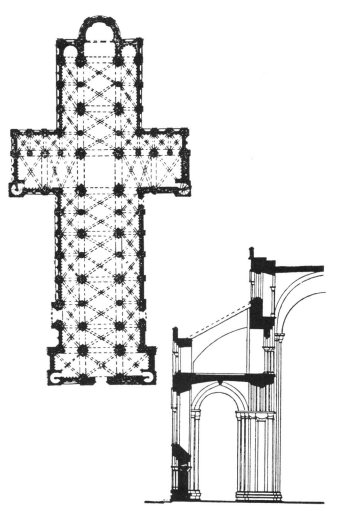

Plan of the Cathedral of Durham, and Section Showing Vaulting and Buttressing

The Last Judgment, *Gislebertus, Tympanum of the Main Portal of the Cathedral of Autun, ca. 1130–1135*

arms. It might be to supply horses or provisions, armor, or treasure for whatever purpose the lord wanted it. There was no concept of nationality, no loyalty possible except that of the vassal for his lord, and no crime worse than breaking the feudal oath of fealty. The usual fief was land, though it might also take the form of an office, the right to gather tolls, or to build and operate a mill. During the centuries of disruption after the death of Charlemagne, and under threat of Viking attack, many men were willing to give up what precarious freedom they might have enjoyed as independent landowners in exchange for the protection of a powerful overlord.

Since all property passed to the eldest son, there were large numbers of men of knightly class who were without means of support unless they could sell their services as professional warriors to whatever lords would give them employment. Their fortunes were their arms, armor, and fighting skills, and they went wherever there was a hope of spoils. Their entire education was for combat. The ability to read and write was regarded as suspiciously effeminate, if not evidence of dabbling in the black arts. They fought with ferocious intensity, endured incredible hardships, and died bravely. They were often mercilessly cruel to their enemies, and their

loyalties went no farther than to their immediate lord. If they were lucky, they might win a fief for themselves as a reward for services in war.

For those fortunate enough to be born into gentle families, no matter how far down the social scale, the bargain may not have been too bad a one in such troubled times. But for those living on the land, there was no hope of escape from lives of grinding poverty and exploitation that make many forms of outright slavery seem mild by contrast. As serfs they were bound to the land, without rights or property. They had to till the lord's fields, gather his crops, and cut his wood. They had to grind their grain at his mill and pay him for the privilege. They could not leave the village or marry without his permission, and they had no property to bequeath to their children, who also belonged to the lord. They could find refuge in entering the church as monks or nuns, or become candidates for the priesthood, only upon paying the lord a heavy indemnity for the loss of their labor in his fields. Almost all of Europe lived on the verge of starvation. It is no wonder, then, that there were peasant uprisings, born of desperation and quelled with cruel violence. One has only to study the Last Judgment over the door of the abbey Church of Conques, and that sculptured by Gislebertus on the portal at Autun, to sense the dilemma in which men found themselves. They were between the perils and hopelessness of their world and the fear of the eternal damnation that they were told awaited them.

In April of 1095 people watched in terror as shower after shower of meteorites fell upon the earth from spring skies. It was clearly a portent of great moment, and it was interpreted for them the following autumn when Pope Urban II called a council at Clermont in Auvergne. "The end of the world is near," he warned. "The days of Antichrist are at hand. If, when he cometh, he finds no Christians in the East, as at this moment there are scarce any such, then there will be no man to stand against him . . . . Hitherto," he told the listening knights and barons, "ye have waged unjustifiable warfare, slaying each other and sometimes wielding mad weapons for the sake merely of greed or of pride, whereby ye have earned everlasting death and the ruin of eternal damnation. Now we set before you wars which have in themselves the glorious reward of martyrdom, and the halo of present and everlasting fame." To those who died fighting to recover Jerusalem he promised a martyr's crown. He forgave all debts to those who would go,

and protected by a mighty curse their families and lands from harassment or seizure.

The hundreds assembled in the bitter November cold greeted his message with shouts as the will of God. They vowed to take the cross, and set about making plans for the expedition that was to start later the following summer and rendezvous at Constantinople, from whence the great invasion was to be launched. In the meantime, a strange monk wandered through the villages and towns of northern France, bringing the news of Pope Urban's declaration in a torrent of passionate words that aroused his hearers to hysteria. A mysteriously compelling figure, with beard flowing in the wind like some Old Testament prophet, Peter the Hermit promised them in the Pope's name remission of their sins and sure entrance for their souls to paradise if they followed him to the Holy Land.

Here was escape from disease and suffering, from hopeless poverty and unrelenting exploitation. So men pledged themselves to a new seigneur, to Christ Himself. Early the following year they were joined by German peasants, some of them led by geese and goats, animals sacred among their recently pagan forebears. Probably about forty thou-

Detail of the Autun Tympanum, Gislebertus

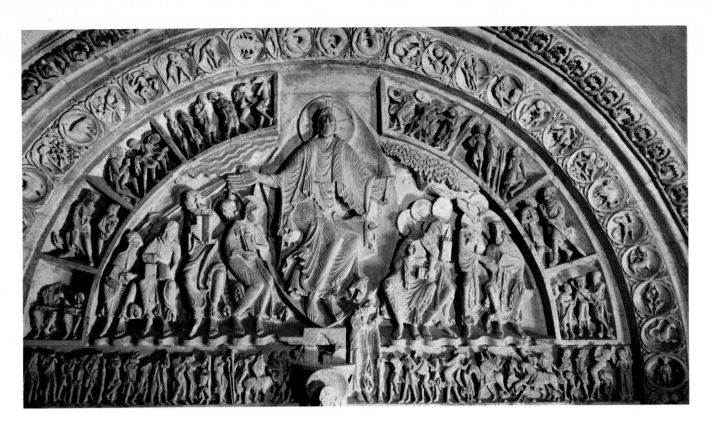

The Mission of the Apostles, *Tympanum of the Main Portal of the Entrance Porch, Church of St. Mary Magdalene, Vézelay, 1120–1132*

sand strong, the first wave, the Crusade of the Peasants, followed Peter the Hermit and a strange knight known as Walter the Penniless eastward across Europe and down the Balkan Peninsula. They saw every stranger as a Saracen, and they slaughtered all they saw, starting with the Jews: were they not infidels, and had not the Pope promised them paradise for killing the infidel?

In a tide of violence they flowed southeastward, leaving a devastated countryside in their bloody wake, finally straggling into Constantinople during the months of summer. There they set fires and looted churches until the Emperor, with Byzantine subtlety, assisted them in crossing the Bosporus, where the Turks almost annihilated them. According to the account left by the Emperor's daughter, an appropriate monument was raised to their victory, a "mountain of bones, most conspicuous in height and breadth and depth." Of those who survived, most were sold into slavery, though a few managed to cross again into Europe, where the Emperor disarmed them and allowed them to wander northward. Few managed to escape the vengeance of their fellow Christians in Bulgaria and Hungary, whose lands they had so brutally ravaged a few months before. Walter the Penniless was dead, and Peter the Hermit, whose admonitions they had

scorned, had disappeared, broken in spirit at the perversion of the crusade by the cruelty and greed of those who followed him and then repudiated his leadership.

A second wave, the Crusade of the Princes, followed, perhaps a half million knights and soldiers in four contingents. The first was led by Count Raymond of Toulouse, the second by the gigantic Godfrey of Bouillon and his two brothers, the third by Hugh, brother of the King of France, Robert of Normandy, the eldest son of William the Conqueror, Robert, Count of Flanders, and Stephen, Count of Chartres, who had larger estates than the King himself. The fourth was commanded by the ablest leader among them, Bohemund, the Norman Prince of Tarentum in Southern Italy. Knights and men-at-arms from all over Europe took the cross, vowing to free the Holy Land from the Moslems, but they little reckoned the cost. After three years of heavy fighting, and cruelty easily matching that of the luckless peasants who had preceded them, Godfrey was elected King of Jerusalem. Bohemund had made himself Prince of Antioch, and others had carved estates for themselves from the western shores of Asia Minor, ruled from immense, fortified citadels.

There northerners who had known only the hardships of the campaign and of living in verminous and drafty castles, as bleak and malodorous as barns, and who knew no medicine except the most rough-and-ready treatment of battle wounds, found themselves in a civilized country. Houses had fresh running water piped in from springs. Windows had shutters for protection against the heat that necessitated not only a change in costume to that of the Saracens but also a change in the life of restless and violent activity that they had always followed. They were amazed at the skill of Moslem physicians and delighted in the variety of foods available to them, so different from the spoiled meat and bread of moldy bran to which many were accustomed to resort during the long northern winters.

The Near East was a land of unbelievable luxury and of constant danger. Rivalry among the Christians led to plots involving the infidel enemy as well as fellow crusaders. There were quick fortunes to be made, followed often by an even quicker death by assassination. Their ideas of the Moslem underwent profound change from the childish notions with which they had left their homes. They found the Turk as strong and brave a fighter as they themselves, and their superior in manners, education, and many skills. With the unaccustomed luxury, purpose weakened, disunity increased, and the success of Saracen counterblows jeopardized the Latin principalities.

On the last day of March, 1146, the great St. Bernard himself preached a second crusade to King Louis VII and a multitude that had assembled on the hillside at Vézelay in Burgundy. Above them on the hilltop rose the basilica dedicated to St. Mary Magdalene. Over the main portal, less than a quarter of a century before, an unknown sculptor had carved a majestic Christ in what is perhaps the finest of all Romanesque tympanums, as such overdoor panels are called. Its subject was especially pertinent to St. Bernard's message, for it shows Christ's mission to the apostles, who are gathered on either side. Their figures are expressively contorted as if by the electric immediacy and overwhelming significance of their task to take the word of the gospel to the uttermost ends of the earth. The gaunt, angular form of the Savior, enhanced by rippling draperies, imparts a sense of movement to the gesture through which the apostles receive the Holy Spirit from His outstretched hands. The small compartments above and the lintel below include all the heathen races of the earth, interpreted with medieval fantasy. The semicircular molding above has medallions with the scenes of the labors of the months interspersed with the signs of the zodiac to show that there is no limit in either time or space to a Christian's duty.

Engraved Brass Tomb of Sir Roger de Trumpington, a Veteran of the Fourth Crusade, 1270

King Arthur and His Knights, *on the Portal of the Cathedral of Modena, Italy*

Perhaps few of St. Bernard's vast audience paid much attention to the tympanum, for the Second Crusade brought a further horde of savage and illiterate northerners southward where they massacred as many Greeks and other Christians as they did Saracens before their defeat. By the time of the Third Crusade, brought on by the Saracens' capture of Jerusalem in 1187, the bravery and chivalry of the Moslem ruler, Saladin, put to shame the cruelty and the treachery of the Christian leaders, King Richard the Lion-Hearted of England, King Philip Augustus of France, and the Emperor Frederick Barbarossa.

The Fourth Crusade reached a climax of perfidy in 1204 with the capture and sack of the Christian city of Constantinople by the crusaders under the influence of the wily Venetian Doge, Enrico Dandolo. Dandolo sought to put an end to his city's main rival in the Eastern trade, cynically diverting the forces sent by the Pope against the Saracens by appeals to their own greed.

The era of crusading may be said to have ended in 1212 when a horde of children, led by a twelve-year-old shepherd, Stephen of Cloyes, trudged southward to Marseilles, hoping to walk dry-shod across the Mediterranean as Moses had crossed the Red Sea. There merchants offered them passage to the Holy Land, and took them instead to Algiers, where they were sold into slavery among the Saracens. Only one of thirty thousand French children is known ever to have returned, and that only after eighteen years of captivity, while perhaps two thousand of the twenty thousand German children finally reached home.

For generations thereafter, there was talk and sometimes action about reconquering the Holy Land from the heathen, but the compulsive migrations of peoples with which the Middle Ages had started so many centuries before had finally reached an end in the irrational explosion, essentially barbarian in spirit, of the Crusades. The heathen, far more tolerant and enlightened than most of the Christians, allowed pilgrims to go to Jerusalem, provided they went in peace. The Saracens proved too good customers and business associates to risk losing through war, and in Asia Minor there developed an easy relationship among Moslem, Christian, and Jew that might well have provided an example for a yet unenlightened Europe.

"The triumphs of the Crusades," the distinguished historian Sir Steven Runciman has written, "were the triumphs of faith. But faith without wisdom is a dangerous thing.... There was so much courage and so little honor, so much devotion and so little understanding. High ideals were besmirched by cruelty and greed, enterprise and endurance by a blind and narrow self-righteousness; and the Holy War itself was nothing more than a long act of intolerance in the name of God, which is a sin against the Holy Ghost."

As a result of the Crusades, the West was never to be the same again. In the East many a savage northerner caught a glimpse of a civilization he had never dreamed of. He learned not only how to make Greek fire and gunpowder so that his subsequent wars could be yet more destructive, but also how to make paper, a Chinese invention introduced into Europe by Arab prisoners, which made printing possible. He learned the use of the compass, which enables him to make his voyages of exploration that led him to a new world. From the Arabs he learned of medicine and science, as well as mathematics and engineering. To the Arabs he was indebted for the survival of such ancient learning of the Greeks and Romans as his own superstition had not destroyed. From the East came silks and cottons for clothing, foodstuffs to the great improvement of his diet, and new habits of cleanliness to the equal improvement of his health. His churches treasured intricate goldsmith work and glassware from Arab lands and farther east, as well as rich vestments made from damask, which takes its name from Damascus. Carved ivories and illuminations from the skilled hands

of Byzantine-trained artists changed his concepts of form and space from the flat, patterned designs of the Northern tradition to the three-dimensionality of the Classic past. The rich heritage of design and color from China, Persia, and the Levant flowed into Europe through the Moslems of Sicily and Spain as well as the Near East, to the enrichment of both castle and church, whose bleak walls were now covered with tapestries or painted in fresh colors. Out of the centuries of strife and suffering gradually emerged a different world. The growing enthusiasm for the adoration of the Virgin tempered cruelty with compassion. Law began to be substituted for the brute force that had been too long the only recognized source of power.

In all this development the arts played a major part. Pilgrims on the Road of St. James heard the jongleurs sing of the deeds of the paladins of Charlemagne and of their magnanimity and honor to friend and foe alike. The tales of King Arthur and his knightly companions of the Round Table, with their selfless devotion to right, were carved on the portals of churches beside the figures of saints and martyrs. They served as models of manhood that an increasing number of the well-born tried to emulate. The overwhelming faith that had led to the horrors of the Crusades was turned to the building of the great cathedrals by whole communities, with architects, engineers, masons, carpenters, sculptors, glaziers, metalworkers, painters, and other craftsmen all working together in dedicated effort.

The Cathedral of Durham, England, 1093–1133

VII   THE GOTHIC CLIMAX

From the earliest days of the Frankish kings, the Abbey of St.-Denis near Paris has had a special significance. St.-Denis is the patron saint of France. It was under his banner, the Oriflamme, that the French kings went forth to battle. Charlemagne and his father, Pepin, had been consecrated kings of France in the abbey dedicated to him. It was the burial place of Pepin, as of Charles the Hammer, victor over the Moslems at Tours, and of Charlemagne's successor, the emperor Charles the Bald, who had been its abbot in name. For centuries the abbey had been enriched with pious donations until its domains stretched for miles, and its revenues made its abbot, often of royal family, one of the grandees of the realm. Today its battered gray walls reflect the grimness of one of the most poverty-stricken parts of France, a grimy industrial suburb that sprawls like a sinister stain across a fair land. But in the twelfth century, protected by heavy battlemented walls, the towers of the royal abbey rose above a great stretch of fertile fields that swept down to the banks of the smooth-flowing Seine.

Early in the twelfth century an unknown peasant boy, who had been born in 1081, short and slight in figure but with a burning ambition to rise in the church, was enrolled as a student in the famous school of St.-Denis. He had as a fellow classmate the prince who later succeeded to the throne as Louis VI. Early showing his extraordinary ability, Suger had a meteoric career. In 1122, at the age of forty-one, he found himself Abbot of St.-Denis, a man who controlled three cities, seventy-four villages, twenty-nine manors, over a hundred

Abbey of St.-Denis, near Paris, 1137–1144, from an old print. Archives Photographiques — Paris

parishes, chapels, and hostels, thousands of acres of woodland and arable fields, vineyards, and farms. But he found the affairs of the abbey in incredible disarray. Sacred objects from the treasury were in pawn for debt, the monks were uncontrolled, and the very fabric of the ancient church was cracked and crumbling.

With his customary energy, Suger set to work to put things to rights, and in less than ten years the abbey was flourishing. Then he could start the project dearest to his heart, the rebuilding of its church in a form worthy of its royal dignity as the center of Christendom in France, the fount of the power of the crown. To Suger, monarchy was a sacred thing. The king of France, like King David in the Bible, was the anointed of the Lord. Ever since Charlemagne had been crowned by the Pope as Christ's vicar on earth, this concept had been the basis of royal power in France. Suger's twin ambitions were to strengthen the position of the king, disputed by noblemen with greater lands and revenues than he, in order to unify France, and to build up the greatness of the Abbey of St.-Denis. By doing the one, he believed, he was inevitably also accomplishing the other.

Abbot Suger sent out invitations to master craftsmen in all parts of Europe, and summoned workmen from far and wide to commence the reconstruction of the church that was to provide the direction for European architecture for centuries to come. Work began in 1137, and as it progressed, Suger, with his architects and engineers, evolved the style that in a later era was disparagingly called Gothic because of that term's connotations of barbarism. Today it brings to mind the aspiring kind of building which seems to us to be among the highest expressions of the human spirit. The tall facade of St.-Denis, disfigured and incomplete today, its sculptures broken by the destructive violence of the French Revolution, and without its northern tower that once rose two hundred and seventy-three feet, has so much in common with facades of Norman churches that scholars have shrewdly suggested that the chief architect may have actually been a Norman. Though the arches are roundheaded as in Romanesque architecture, the rising verticality of the Gothic is already there. The lovely rose window is the first of its kind, and the progenitor of all the others since that day. People thronged to take part in the pious work, and it progressed so fast that the facade, complete with portals sculptured with a host of saints and prophets, was sufficiently

finished to be dedicated on a warm June day in 1140.

Immediately, work started on the choir to transform it completely into a subtle composition of tall columns (twelve in number to symbolize the apostles) bearing ribbed vaults whose profile took the unmistakable form of the Gothic arch. It was at this moment that the Gothic style was born. All the ingredients were there—soaring lightness and weightless grace, a cage of slender stone elements whose glass walls flooded the interior with glowing illumination. Many changes have taken place but scholars have been able to reconstruct on paper the entire choir, while its arcading and double ambulatory, or processional way, still remains as Suger left it. Curving around the east end, it passes before seven shallow chapels radiating outward from the center, the piers between them supported by buttresses on the exterior of the church. None

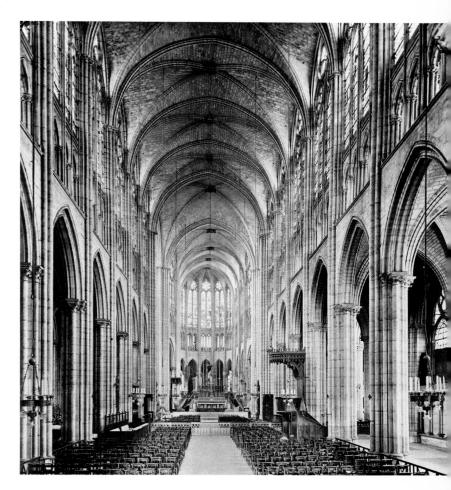

Nave of the Abbey of St.-Denis, Looking Toward the Choir, 1140–1144

of the great Romanesque churches had attempted this double-aisled apse, nor had any of them tried the daring replacement of masonry walls with stained-glass windows as did Suger.

Three years and three months later (the symbolic identification of the threes with the Trinity came naturally to Suger), the church was completed. On the second Sunday in June, 1144, a procession led by the King and his beautiful Queen, the head-strong Eleanor of Aquitaine, the Queen Mother, princes, archbishops, prelates, noblemen and ladies, and a crowd of knights, burghers, and citizens wound its way from Paris across fields green with early summer to the consecration of the new sanctuary sacred to the Apostle of the French and the patron of France. At the main altar in the ambulatory, and in the more ruggedly vaulted crypt beneath, the nineteen prelates, "decorous in white vestments," according to Suger's own account, "splendidly arrayed in pontifical miters, walked round and round . . . and invoked the name of God so piously that the King and the attending nobility believed themselves to behold a chorus celestial rather than terrestrial, a ceremony divine rather than human." It was a high point in the life of the peasant boy whom the church had "raised," as he had written, "a beggar from the dunghill," to the equal of any man in France. He was twice to be regent of the kingdom while the monarch was away on the Crusades. He stood at the right hand of the throne. His wise and practical advice, based upon his peasant's instinctive knowledge of human nature, met with universal respect. His influence upon history was great, but his impact on the arts was incalculable. He was responsible for the creation of the Gothic style in architecture. His ideas and dreams for the church inspired generations down through the centuries till the Age of Reason ended in its unreasoning outbursts of violence in the French Revolution. What eighteenth-century architects had not already destroyed, the mob did. Today we must look elsewhere to see the embodiment of Suger's idea of raising men's minds and spirits "from the material to the immaterial" so that when they saw the beauty and the splendor of the altars, with crosses studded with precious stones and golden reliquaries enameled in brilliant colors, their throughts would rise to splendors and beauties beyond anything that can be known on earth. Like the anonymous writer whom the Middle Ages thought to be no less a personage than St.-Denis himself, Suger believed that harmony, based on just relations of numbers and proper proportions, was the source of beauty, and that light was itself a gift of God. When the light of day filled the glass-walled sanctuary of his abbey church with a luminous flood of radiant color, it became a symbol of the light of truth and of the True Light, or Christ Himself. The beauty has gone from St.-Denis, brooding amidst the sadness of the slums. But the beauty and the splendor that Suger loved have been miraculously preserved for us — despite wars and revolutions, and, as destructive, the cruel hands of later improvers — in the cathedrals that are the greatest glory of France.

The age of cathedral-building began with Suger's reconstruction of St.-Denis and lasted for more than a century. By about 1250 the momentum was starting to flag, and though Gothic buildings continued to be constructed for more than two hundred years, in an era finally brought to a close by the outbreak of the Hundred Years' War in 1337, the greatest of them were substantially completed during the thirteenth century.

During this period eighty cathedrals, five hundred large churches, and thousands of parish churches and chapels were built, until there was one building for every two hundred persons. In the larger cities the cathedrals could contain the entire population on feast days and special holy days. The cathedrals were the expression of pride of the city dwellers, men who had won their freedom from feudal bondage and who held the charter of the community direct from the king or ruling prince. Meeting in council, they could elect their own officers to rule them. To be a citizen, a freeman of a city, was a privilege much sought after. It meant independence to follow one's trade or craft, subject only to the laws of the commune and rules of the guild which regulated that craft in the interest of quality, fair trade, and protection of both the craftsman and his client. Lucky was the serf, fleeing the vengeance of a domineering lord, who could remain a year and a day in a city, for then he was a free man.

The cities were founded on commerce and grew from trading stations at crossroads, at the mouths of rivers, beside good harbors, or along the old Roman roads that became again the routes of trade. Europe's population, decimated by war and disease, was not large. Paris in the twelfth century was one of the biggest cities in the Western world and had only fifty to sixty thousand souls. This number included the unruly horde of students from all parts of Europe who gave the name of Latin

Quarter to that part of the Left Bank where their classes were held, because that was the universal language in which they carried out their studies, wrote their books, and argued long and vociferously with one another. Only in the freedom of a city could a university exist, and thus the cities replaced the monasteries as intellectual centers and became centers of trade as well. A brilliant teacher attracted students from afar. Cities vied with one another for the privilege of playing host to a university, though the solid burghers must often have questioned the judgment that allowed a penniless, roistering mob in their midst, quick to riot and ready to turn an abstract philosophical argument into a street brawl. Often protected by the church and granted certain rights by the city, the great universities, like that of Paris, were divided into nations and offered courses in theology, canon law, arts, and medicine. Lectures were held wher-

ever there was room—in a cloister, in a guild hall, or in the open air—and students were free to come and go at will.

Out of the vital ferment of the medieval university grew the crowning intellectual achievement of the Middle Ages, the *Summa Theologica* of St. Thomas Aquinas. In this great work the brilliant churchman summed up the world's knowledge and reconciled what was known of the Classic past with the teachings of the church, a blending of the pagan and the Christian worlds. In it St. Thomas created an edifice that was the equivalent in the realm of thought to the great cathedrals. For just as the *Summa Theologica* gave form to the patterns of faith, the cathedrals realized them in three dimensions. For a cathedral, as the great French scholar Émile Mâle has pointed out, is "the image of the world." Its sculptures and windows illustrate the Creation, the Fall of Man, his redemption through Christ's suffering and crucifixion, and the assurance of life hereafter.

Significantly, almost all the great cathedrals were dedicated to the Virgin as the Queen of Heaven, the all-forgiving benefactor of sinful humanity.

Thirteenth- and fourteenth-century fortifications of Aigues-Mortes, founded in 1240 by St. Louis in the Rhône delta. From here the king embarked on the disastrous crusades of 1248 and 1270.

Cathedral of Chartres

The cult of the Virgin did much to civilize the later Middle Ages. Her church was a sanctuary and refuge for the oppressed and the suffering. Men and women dedicated their devotion to her, and armored warriors shouted her name as they charged into battle. The great St. Bernard, who had preached the Second Crusade on the hillside at Vézelay, and whose order of monks, the Cistercians, carried his ideals of austere and unembellished architectural beauty, the very opposite of his contemporary Suger's, into all parts of Europe, composed countless hymns to her. To her he dedicated each of the hundreds of monastic churches built by his followers.

The first of the great Gothic cathedrals was Notre-Dame of Chartres, a city that traditionally was the home of the Virgin. There was an ancient legend that in late pagan times the populace worshiped a female deity who had given virgin birth to a savior son in a grotto reputed to lie somewhere beneath the present cathedral's pavement. The Bishop of Chartres in the middle of the twelfth century was a friend of Abbot Suger, and was well aware of the revolutionary new developments at St.-Denis. In 1145 he began construction on a new fabric. A half century later, fire destroyed all but the facade. The townsfolk were in despair until they learned that their most precious relic, the garment believed to have been worn by the Vir-

gin when her Son was born, had miraculously survived the flames. It was clear then to any Frenchman of the twelfth century that it was somehow ordained that the church be rebuilt with yet increased grandeur.

From miles around people came, lords and laborers, craftsmen, women, and even children. "Who has ever seen!" exclaimed a Norman abbot in a letter to brother monks in an English abbey. "Who has ever heard tell, in times past, that powerful princes of the world, that men brought up in honor and in wealth, that nobles, men and women, have bent their proud and haughty necks to the harness of carts, and that, like beasts of burden, they have dragged to the abode of Christ these wagons, loaded with wines, grains, oil, stone, wood, and all that is necessary for the wants of life, or for the construction of the church. . . . When they have reached the church, they arrange the wagons about it like a spiritual camp, and during the whole night they celebrate the watch by hymns and canticles. On each wagon they lighted tapers and lamps. They place there the infirm and the sick, and bring them the precious relics of the Saints for their relief."

The actual construction of the church, however, was carried out by an army of trained men: masons, carpenters, mortarers, glaziers, blacksmiths, quarrymen, and laborers, under the direction of architects

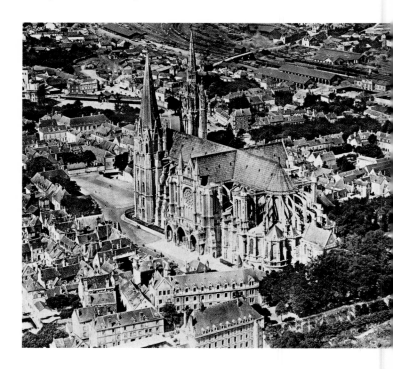

Cathedral of Chartres from the Air

Facade of the Cathedral of Chartres, mid-12th century, the Rose Window 1200, the Northern Spire 1507

Windows were donated by guilds and princes, and often portrayed the patron saints of each. Though details of hands and faces might be actually painted on the glass with bold and simple strokes, the windows are made up of countless small pieces arranged so that the lead reinforces the design of the whole. The result is less an art of stained glass than of painting with light. The achievements of the generations of Romanesque artists who had perfected the medium went into the windows of the Gothic cathedrals. The result is the magic of light that so moved Abbot Suger and that we find so impressive today.

If one follows the Pilgrimage Road from Paris sixty miles away, as did students in the medieval university, and as their descendants were said to have done even down to the beginning of this century, the gray towers of the cathedral can be seen for miles across the golden wheat fields of

and engineers. Pious donations for the work came from as far away as Spain, and the fabric rose from the ashes of the earlier church with amazing speed. By 1220 it was substantially complete.

More than two generations of workers lived on the cathedral site or at the quarries at Berchères-l'Évêque, five miles away, where the very hard, fine-grained stone was cut. The masons had their timber lodge, where they lived and worked, the original of the lodges of Freemasonry of later times. There the sculptors carved the figured capitals and columnar statues of saints and prophets for the portals, later to be brightly colored and gilded by the painters.

In other sheds the glaziers worked at oversize tables, large enough so that an entire window could be laid out at once. There they cut the pieces of colored glass that were fitted together with flexible lead strips and fastened to an iron grid for strength to create what has been called the most beautiful glass in the world.

Central Portal of the Cathedral of Chartres, 1145

The Virgin and Child, *from the Tympanum of the South Portal of the Main Facade, Cathedral of Chartres. Archives Photographiques—Paris*

The Ascension of Christ, *Tympanum of the North Portal of the Main Facade, Cathedral of Chartres. Archives Photographiques—Paris*

the Beauce. For hours the road runs straight as a die between rows of tall trees which shelter wayfarers from the summer sun. As one gets closer, the tall body of the church can be seen above the cluster of low buildings of the ancient city. Even walking through the narrow, winding streets, one rarely loses sight of the towers that serve as beacons for the pilgrim. Today the ancient houses have been cleared from about the walls of the church; but once, so precious was the land within the circuit of the city's fortifications that all sorts of buildings were constructed against it, hiding its lower parts, and emphasizing its loftiness. For as one enters the square before the facade, its soaring height is breathtaking.

As is the case with most of the cathedrals, Chartres was never really finished, and there is great disparity in date, and thus in style, among various parts. For example, the lower of the two towers, that to the right, has foundations that may date back to before the First Crusade, while its spire was built between 1145 and 1170. The northern tower, to the left, was not started before 1110. That part of it which rises above the height of the facade was not carried out till after 1500, during the very years when Michelangelo's superb dome for St. Peter's in Rome, one of the greatest monuments of the Renaissance, was rising over a city where a new era had already begun.

The central, or royal, portal is dominated by the sculptured tympanum of the Savior surrounded by the symbolic beasts of the Evangelists, the motive of Christ in Majesty, based on the vision of Ezekiel. Serene and benign, Christ's hand is raised to bless all who enter. Beneath, on either side of all three portals, stand the tall columnar figures of the Old Testament kings, queens, and prophets to suggest the continuity of the church with the New Testament as the fulfillment of the Old. The tympanum to the left shows the Christ of the Ascension rising heavenward between angels, while that to the right has the Virgin seated with the Child in her lap as Queen of Heaven.

On going into the church, one enters a world different from that of our noisy and material age. The nave rises more than a hundred and twenty feet above the pavement, its great height emphasized by the slender, clustered colonnettes that carry the eye upward to trace their joining with the ribs of the vault which meet finally at the apex far above. Chartres has been fortunate enough to retain more of its original glass than any other cathedral. Standing under the crossing, one can turn to see each of the three great rose windows, the earliest over the entrance doors to the west, and the later ones at the ends of the transepts. High up on the walls are the windows of the clerestory, mostly given by churchmen and nobles, while

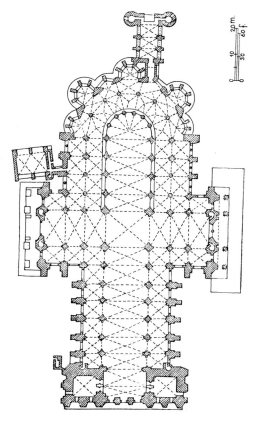

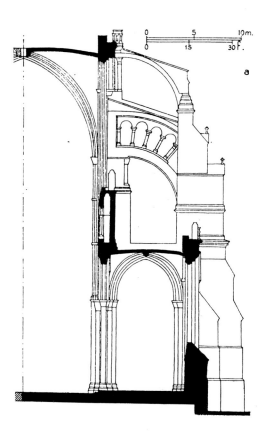

Plan of the Cathedral of Chartres

Section of the Cathedral of Chartres

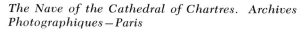

The Nave of the Cathedral of Chartres. Archives Photographiques—Paris

many of those along the aisles were presented by the guilds whose members so often congregated close by. All the windows glow with rich blues and reds that have never been equaled. The ordinary light of day is filtered and diffused by the huge areas of colored glass, warming the cold, gray stone to life, penetrating the spacious interior with slanting shafts, and transforming the whole into an otherworldly atmosphere "pervaded," in Suger's words, by the wonderful and uninterrupted light of most radiant windows."

Inlaid in the pavement is the only remaining example of the labyrinth that appeared on many of the great cathedral floors. Contained in a circle limited in diameter only by the width of the nave, it is a narrow, patterned path whose winding course the faithful followed on their knees, prayerfully making their way to the center, thus figuratively completing a pilgrimage to the Holy Land. The idea of the labyrinth extends backward into the mists of man's beginnings. Labyrinths appear in connection with megalithic temples, and in the Palace of Minos at Cnossus in Crete. Recalling

Labyrinth in the Pavement at the Nave, Chartres.
Archives Photographiques—Paris

Knocker, Sanctuary Door, North Porch of the
Cathedral of Durham, England

the ancient legend of the latter, medieval chroniclers refer to the plaque in the center of the cathedral labyrinths as "the House of Daedalus," the imaginary inventor who is thought to have designed the labyrinth in Crete to contain the Minotaur, the bull-headed monster that Theseus vanquished. But on the cathedral plaques were inscribed not only the names but often also the likenesses of the architects who had created the church, thus conferring upon them immortality symbolized by the identification of the plaque with Jerusalem, the Heavenly City.

Capital with Foliage and Winged Monsters, Cathedral of Rheims, France. Archives Photographiques—Paris

The curious mixture of echoes half heard from the Classic past, transformed by centuries and infused with pious legend and Christian faith, is typical of much of the Middle Ages. It was a time that envisioned the fabulous monsters, the minions of Satan that lurk in the foliage of a sculptured capital, pose as a knocker on a sanctuary door, or that, as gargoyles, serve as waterspouts from the corners of tower and parapet. As an "image of the world," the cathedral showed the pagans of far places as pig-snouted, or with batlike ears, or headless and with eyes and mouth in their chests, according to the tall traveler's tales that had come down through centuries. Fact and fantasy merged, and miracles were commonplace. All had a part in the cathedral, as an expression of the eternal struggle of man for redemption.

In the tall and stalwart St. Theodore of the South Portal, man saw the ideal of the knight as a gentle but fearless soldier of the Lord. In the Annunciation of the Nativity of Christ to the Shepherds, he could take comfort that the lowly were the first to receive the glad tidings. In the Adoration of the Kings, he saw the exalted humbled by the mystery of the Nativity. Christ's humiliation and suffering before His crucifixion ennobled the woes and hurts of man's own uncertain existence. In the dignity of the prophets of the Old Testament, he recognized the antiquity of the knowledge of the inevitable coming of Christ. This fulfillment,

The Annunciation to the Shepherds, *Detail of the
South Portal of the Facade of Chartres*

July Sharpening a Scythe, *from the* Labors of the Months, *Cathedral of Notre-Dame, Paris*

man experienced again and again as the church celebrated its progression throughout the feasts of the canonical year from the Annunciation to the Virgin, through the joyous birth, to the tragedy of the crucifixion, to the glory of the resurrection.

The saints were a part of it as well. The reliefs of the Labors of the Months, the planting, pruning, harvesting, and all the tasks so basic to life in an agricultural age, were regulated by the saints. Mowing was started on St. Barnabas' Day. Barley had to be sowed on St. George's Day because by St. Mark's Day it was too late. St. Genevieve cured fevers, St. Sebastian offered protection against the plague, and St. Christopher guarded the traveler on his journey. The oxen were under the protection of St. Cornelius, the pigs under the care of St. Anthony, and the sheep in the keeping of St. Saturninus.

Harvesting Grapes, *one of a series of Capitals showing the Labors of the Months, Cathedral of Rheims, France. Archives Photographiques—Paris*

Each guild had its patron saint. The masons celebrated St. Thomas' Day with a procession and a feast, while the tanners celebrated St. Bartholomew's Day because the martyrdom of that saint took the grisly form of being skinned alive. The emblems and figures of these saints appeared in the windows given by the guilds.

All was made an immediate part of life by the

Christ in Majesty *from the* Tree of Jesse *Window, Chartres. Archives Photographiques—Paris*

brightly colored carvings on the churches as well as the words of the priests, but they were brought vividly to life by the mystery plays that took place at major feasts of the church, especially Christmas and Easter. Then on the cathedral steps or in the cloister all the citizens of the city, with many others who came in from outlying districts, saw enacted the episodes from Scripture. In a series of rough stage sets the Nativity took place, with angels chanting from a wooden balcony above. The shepherds came with their sheep, and then the Wise Men, the Magi, dressed in costumes of fantastic richness, often using borrowed vestments from the cathedral treasury, topped by towering turbans. Then came the episodes of Christ's life and suffering. Throughout, the Devil was always lurking near, complete with tail and horns, tempting Christ with dominion of the world, plaguing the souls of the dead, trying to upset the balance of the scales in which each was weighed by St. Michael at the terrible time of the Last Judgment. At last he was driven screaming into the mouth of Hell, which belched forth real smoke and flames, by the forces of righteousness. All was as immediate and constant a part of life as were the changing seasons whose succession was marked by the celebrations of the canonical year.

The cathedrals belonged to the people. In most cases the bishop or archbishop controlled only the sanctuary. The rest was under the jurisdiction of the chapter of canons, priests who were his assistants in carrying out the various duties of the diocese. Under their dean, the chapter of canons was responsible for the fabric of the church, its construction and repair, its treasury and management of revenues. A bishop might be a leader in a campaign for rebuilding, but it was the chapter of

Christ Blessing, *Central Portal, 1230, Amiens, France*

*St. Theodore, on the South Portal, Chartres, ca.
1215–1220*

The Blue Virgin, *Stained-Glass Window, Chartres.
Archives Photographiques — Paris*

canons that, generation after generation, carried
the work ahead, planning, financing, overseeing,
completing. And all of the cathedral except the
sanctuary was almost always open to the populace.
Many a medieval city did not have a city hall because the councilors met in the cathedral's nave.
Guilds also sometimes met there. Booths were
set up inside the church at the times of the great
fairs that were so important to the revenues of the
community as well as of the cathedral. Every
aspect of life was infused with faith, and the daily
work in the fields and vineyards, in the workshops
or lodges, was sanctified. Labor was a form of
prayer, and nothing was undertaken without in-
voking God or His saints. Thus the bustle of the
marketplace could enter the very structure of the
cathedral just as the faith that had built the cathedral entered the very fabric of life of the people in
all its variety of activity and responsibility. And
on feast days all the people crowded into the nave.
There were no seats or benches, and noblemen,
burghers, peasants, and royalty itself jostled together in the press of those taking part in the
celebration.

VIII THE FLOWERING OF MEDIEVAL ITALY

There was change in the air in thirteenth-century Italy. It was a time of contrasts, of creation and destruction, of hope and despair. No one person better exemplified its contradictory qualities than the only emperor since the fall of Rome to grow up and spend his life in that country. Frederick II came of the house of Hohenstaufen, which originated in Swabia in southwest Germany. Through his Norman mother he inherited the kingdom of Sicily, and he married a Spanish princess of the dynasty of Aragon that ruled Naples. He was educated in Palermo, the Sicilian capital, under tutors chosen by the Pope, who was determined that a young prince of his potential importance must be properly indoctrinated to cooperate with papal political ambitions. Apparently such precautions were in vain, however, because Frederick absorbed all the sophistication of the polyglot Norman court, with its Greek scholars and courtiers, its luxury, and elaborate Oriental customs. By the time, in his mid-twenties, he was crowned Holy Roman Emperor by Pope Innocent III, he was master of six languages and the arts of intrigue as well. He surrounded himself with the most brilliant group of poets, scientists, and artists he could find. He was outrageously guilty of what was in the eyes of the orthodox of the day the heinous sin of tolerance, for he welcomed Jews, Arabs, Mongols, and Christians alike. He avidly studied such forbidden subjects as pagan philosophy and literature of classical times, and the works of Islamic authors. Furthermore, his behavior was scarcely calculated to reassure the Pope of his devout submission to papal control. As a result his admirers called him *stupor mundi*, ("the wonder of the world"), and the

Castel del Monte, Apulia, Italy, 13th century

church considered him Antichrist, while historians have dubbed him the first modern man. Highly intelligent, imaginative, ruthless, he had a questioning mind devoid of superstition. As one writer described him, "he lived like a caliph, ruled like a Caesar, and considered himself an Italian sovereign destined to reconquer Rome and make it the center of a renewed Christian and Roman empire."

Frederick founded universities at Naples and Palermo, was an enthusiastic patron of music and the arts, and in a period when most rulers were illiterate, was a poet as well as a linguist. His passion for falconry led him to construct the picturesque octagonal Castel del Monte high in the mountains of Apulia, where he and his courtiers could pursue the sport. He also was the author of what is considered the most complete treatise on the subject ever written. Though short and redheaded, he felt himself heir of the ancient emperors, and copied the dress and manners of im-

The Cathedral of Pisa, with the Baptistry and Bell Tower, 1053–1272

Ariel View of the Cathedral of Pisa, with the Bell Tower and Campo Santo

Interior of the Cathedral of Pisa

perial Rome. He erected triumphal arches, and his friends and ministers were portrayed by his sculptors in classical garb, some bearded like Greek philosophers and others crowned with laurel like ancient poets. His court was the center of learning and the arts in the South, and for a brief time it flourished with a splendor not to be seen again in Italy for more than a century.

Frederick's aspiration was to unify the Empire and exercise an enlightened though autocratic rule through trained professional administrators, instead of having to deal with unruly feudal lords and to cajole haughty churchmen. Such an ambition was bound to beget furious opposition. Gradually the Pope, whose temporal powers were thus challenged, managed to unite the Emperor's enemies sufficiently to carry out a long and disastrous conflict ending in Frederick's downfall. The result was not only the destruction of the first Italian imperial dynasty but the political disruption of the country also. Shorn of power, the defeated Emperor died in 1250. His body had not long rested in the immense sarcophagus of red porphyry, still to be seen in the royal chapel of the golden cathedral of Palermo, before it became evident that the struggle had brought about the decline of papal supremacy as well as imperial authority. It was the beginning of the end of the Middle Ages in Italy. But, though the country was politically in a ruinous state, it was to see a flowering of the arts that would have gladdened Frederick's heart,

and that brought an epoch to a triumphant close, and pointed the way into a dramatically different future.

At the Emperor's death the last remains of his court were scattered. One of the artists who had enjoyed his patronage, a thirty-year-old sculptor, Niccolo d' Apulia, made his way with his family, including a five-year-old son named Giovanni, to the free city of Pisa. Lying west of Florence at the mouth of the Arno River, it had long been friendly to the Emperor. There Niccolo saw, on a level stretch of land north of the city, a great cathedral nearing completion. Opposite its colonnaded facade was an immense circular baptistry. To the northeast, a bell tower, later to become the famous leaning tower, was under construction. Niccolo must have admired the remembrance of the Classic past in the sheathing of white marble inlaid with stripes and patterns of dark green, and the echoes of the Arab world in the steeply rising profile of the gleaming dome. Pisa was a maritime power and a trading community, and the handsome complex of cathedral and accompanying buildings was an expression of the city's wealth and pride. The dignity of the superposed blind arcading of the exterior walls was matched in the tall interior,

Pulpit by Niccolo Pisano, Baptistry of the Cathedral of Pisa, Marble, ca. 1250–1260

suggesting an Early Christian basilica in its proportions as well as in the flat ceiling of paneled and gilded wood supported on striped piers reminiscent of buildings in Sicily and the South.

It was natural that the Pisans should have enlisted the skill of such an experienced newcomer as Niccolo. He seems to have embarked at once on a new career in the city-republic that proved so successful that he has ever after been known as Niccolo Pisano, Nicholas the Pisan. For ten years he worked on the elaborate marble pulpit for the baptistry that later ages have come to recognize as a turning point in medieval art. Crouching lions support the dark-red columns that elevate the pulpit, and an eagle with outstretched wings forms the lectern. Remembering the reliefs of ancient sarcophagi that he had studied at the Emperor's court, he designed and sculptured panels with scenes from the Scriptures. Each panel is filled with figures that vie with one another for space within the crowded frame. Each form is realized in bold relief, deeply cut classical draperies emphasizing its solidity.

In the Nativity scene, the Virgin, robed like a Roman matron, reclines in the center. In the foreground, servants bathe the newborn Child, and a seated Joseph, swathed in a toga, looks on from the

Cathedral of Siena, ca. 1270

The Nativity, *Detail from the Pulpit by Niccolo Pisano, Baptistry of the Cathedral of Pisa*

lower left. But not content with the Nativity alone, Niccolo has also portrayed the Annunciation to the left, and beyond the Child in His cradle at the Virgin's side, the Annunciation to the Shepherds takes place, while their sheep graze peacefully to the lower right. Here the sculptor has borrowed not only the forms of Roman art but also the Roman method of treating several subjects simultaneously to tell most effectively as much of the story as possible. Yet the result is obviously not a Roman work. Niccolo has infused it with the spirit of another age and another faith. His is a totally different approach from that of the earlier medieval artists and those working north of the Alps, whose ethereal flamelike figures stress the otherworldliness and remoteness of matters of faith. Instead, by emphasizing the robust solidity of each figure and group, he expresses the essential spirituality of the subject in human and understandable terms, because for men of his era the divine was increasingly a part of life on this earth.

Niccolo's fame traveled far, and he established a dynasty of sculptors that continued for generations. In 1265 he was in Siena, one of the most beautiful medieval cities left in the world. The dome of the great cathedral had been finished the year before. He and his assistants, among them his twenty-year-old son, Giovanni, worked for three years on the monumental octagonal pulpit

A Prophet, *from the Facade of the Cathedral of Siena, by Giovanni Pisano. Victoria and Albert Museum, London*

Fountain by Niccolo and Giovanni Pisano, Perugia, 1275

that dominates a nave made dramatic by the building's construction in alternating courses of stone of contrasting color.

In 1275, for the ancient Etruscan city of Perugia, father and son carved panels in relief of the labors of the months, separated by figures of saints, around the immense fountain in the main square. After his father's death Giovanni sculptured the portals of the Cathedral of Siena. But his masterpiece is fittingly the pulpit that he, in turn, carved for the Cathedral of Pisa, after the turn of the fourteenth century.

The works of both Niccolo and Giovanni became a kind of academy for later artists, painters and sculptors alike. But it is Niccolo whom later times have recognized as the precursor of the age to come. Though the spirit of his work remains entirely medieval, his concern for realism and his return to models from the Classic past to enable him to recapture it, make him the ancestor of the Renaissance. Donatello, Michelangelo, and all the other sculptors of the fifteenth and sixteenth centuries, an era that saw the realization of so many of the forgotten ideals of Frederick II, were Niccolo's spiritual descendants.

Sculptured Detail from the Fountain in Perugia

Pulpit by Niccolo and Giovanni Pisano, 1265–1268, Cathedral of Siena

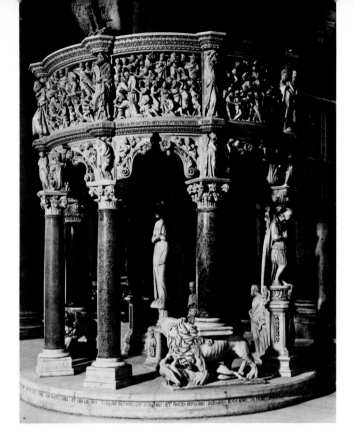

Pulpit by Giovanni Pisano, Cathedral of Pisa, 1302–1310

Twelve miles east of Perugia lies the town of Assisi, sprawled across the lower slopes of Mount Subasio. It looks southward, across the Umbrian plain, green with gardens, vineyards, and olive groves. Above its narrow streets of ancient buildings, still protected by medieval walls, rises a bare hill topped by a fortress. But the focus of the town is not there; nor is it the Cathedral of S. Rufino, with its austerely handsome Romanesque facade and tower; nor is it even the main square, once the forum of the Roman town, and still flanked by the portico of the former temple of Minerva, now the entrance to a church dedicated to the Virgin. Instead, one's footsteps lead toward the massive complex of buildings at the far end of the town, constructed on a shoulder of the hill outthrust westward into the surrounding plain. Looking as though it incorporated the remains of an ancient aqueduct because of the long line of arches that supports it, its mass is crowned by a church whose square tower rises high above the lofty nave. It is one of the world's greatest places of pilgrimage, the Church of St. Francis, whose spirit has dominated Assisi, where he was born and where he lived most of his life, since the beginning of the thirteenth century.

Begun in 1228, just two years after the saint's death, the complex grew, through the next century, into a double church, one above the other, surrounded by a vast monastery of monks of the famous order that he founded. Like the Dominicans, the other great mendicant order, the Franciscans are not cloistered monks. Their lives are dedicated, like his, to poverty, chastity, and obedience, and to the service of God through the service of man. In 1208, in disgust as the dreadful disparity be-

Church of S. Francesco, Assisi, Italy

Madonna Enthroned, *Cimabue, Panel, 12' 7½" ×
7' 4", ca. 1285. Uffizi Gallery, Florence*

tween the self-indulgence of the rich and the
suffering of the poor, Francis suddenly renounced
a life of privilege "to wed," as he expressed it,
"Lady Poverty." He little dreamed that he was
to found an order whose members were to carry
his joyful and selfless ideal throughout the world.
But his followers multiplied as increasing numbers were fired by the flame of his spirit, by his
feeling of brotherhood for everything—the birds
and beasts of field and forest, the moon and the
sun and the stars, and the very trees and plants,
as well as all humanity. It is no wonder that even
during his lifetime, legends clustered about his
name. People told how he tamed the wolf of
Gubbio, which had terrified the countryside until
Francis went into the wilderness, found the wolf's
lair, and brought it back walking docilely by his
side as obedient as a shepherd's faithful dog.

The hymns of praise that Francis composed dis-
pelled the mood of fearfulness and guilt that bur-
dened the souls of men who were all too used to
the strife and cruelty of a world that lived by violence. In his *Canticle of the Sun* he sang the
praises of "our sister, mother earth," and of all
the wonders of the universe, as gifts of God. As
the end of his life drew near, he even thanked God
for "our sister, bodily death, from whom no living
man can flee," for she frees the soul for everlasting
life. His verses on the glories of peace caused
mortal enemies to forgive one another and exchange the symbolic kiss of peace. His message
of joyful acceptance swept through the countryside

as welcome as rain after a long drought. It was
carried by his followers ever farther afield, until
his words and the story of his life became a common heritage of man.

As the basilica rising above his tomb neared
completion, many artists were commissioned to
record the events of the saint's life for all to see.
Among them were the leading painters of the time,
but none was to prove greater than the twenty-
four-year-old Giotto di Bondone. From 1290 until
close to 1300 he painted twenty-eight scenes from
the life of St. Francis along the lower walls of the
nave, below the high windows and between the
clustered piers that support the tall vaulting of
the upper church. No more sympathetic inter-
preter could have been chosen for the task than
the young man who had been born in a remote village in the hilly countryside of the Mugello, northeast of Florence. As a boy he had been apprenticed
to Cimabue, the leading Florentine painter of his

The Miracle of the Spring, *1290–1300, Giotto,
Fresco, Church of S. Francesco, Assisi, Italy*

St. Francis Preaching to the Birds, *1290–1300,*
Giotto, Church of S. Francesco, Assisi, Italy

prayers of the saint. He is surrounded by the birds
to whom Francis preached, his "little brothers of
the air." He becomes a part of the congregation
that celebrated Christmas in the neighboring
town of Greccio with the world's first crèche, with
sculptured figures of those who were present at
the birth of Christ, the Virgin and Child, St. Joseph,
the shepherds with their sheep, and the ox and the
ass.

Giotto presents each event with the same completeness of realization that inspired Francis to
create the crèche of Greccio. The artist shared
the saint's feeling for the joy and beauty of the
world and the brotherhood of all creation. His
painted figures have the same solidity as the rough
sculptures that made up the crèche. And his purpose, like that of Niccolo Pisano, is the same: to
lend weight and immediacy to what had before all
too often been spiritual symbolism remote from
the everyday life of men.

Giotto's greatest works were done in 1305 and
1306 in a small building in Padua called the Arena
Chapel because it had been constructed on the
site of an ancient Roman arena. The frescoes were
commissioned by one Enrico Scrovegni, inheritor
of a fortune amassed through usury, whose con-

generation. He had worked from the age of about
thirteen as an assistant on the frescoes with which
his master adorned the upper walls and the vault
of S. Francesco. They are today so dulled and
damaged by time that they show little of the sense
of scale and austere dignity typical of Cimabue's
work, still Byzantine in design, but with a new
feeling of breadth and humanity in keeping with
the changing spirit of the times. The famous altarpiece of the *Madonna Enthroned,* painted about
1285 and now in the Uffizi Gallery in Florence, is
far better evidence of the style and the quality of
Cimabue's work. It also shows by contrast the
dramatic innovations by which Giotto changed
the whole course of European painting.

In his frescoes Giotto simplified everything,
until nothing remains that does not have a part in
the story. The figures have the same sense of
weight and bulk as those sculptured by Niccolo
Pisano, whose work Giotto must have seen. Set-
tings are reduced to symbolic landscapes or town
views. As if on a narrow stage the action takes
place, parallel to the viewer and at his own eye
level, so that he is included in the painting, which
thus takes on immediate significance for him. He
is present at the miraculous gushing forth of a
spring of pure water from the barren rock at the

The Crèche of Greccio, *1290–1300, Giotto, Fresco,*
Church of S. Francesco, Assisi, Italy

science seems with good reason to have troubled him. But no one could have made more handsome amends, because the frescoes are among the half dozen greatest works of their kind in the world. Around the simple interior, bare as a barn, Giotto painted the scenes of the life and the passion of Christ. The thirty-seven episodes are superbly orchestrated to reach a dramatic climax in the *Last Judgment*. The compositions express even more directly and economically the meaning and the spirit of the whole. The clash of harsh colors of the scene of Christ's *Betrayal* by the kiss of Judas combine with the jagged silhouettes of blazing torches and weapons brandished against the dark sky to emphasize the sinister drama of the event.

The Lamentation, *1305–1306, Giotto, Fresco, Arena Chapel, Padua, Italy*

Never has grief been expressed with greater directness and power than in *The Lamentation* over the body of the crucified Christ. The sky is filled with angels, convulsed with sorrow. The very colors, the acid green and the pale, biting red of garments against the gray of a bleak and desert landscape, give a feeling of despair. The composition focuses on the head of Christ, to the left, held by the sorrow-

ing Virgin. The single tree, its branches bare against the cold sky, not only is another expressive element but also refers to the ancient prophecy that the tree of knowledge, reputed to have died because of the sin of Adam and Eve in the Garden of Eden, would come alive again as a result of Christ's sacrifice upon the cross.

Giotto had a long and productive life and was much honored by his countrymen. He left works in most major Italian cities in fresco, panel-painting, and mosaic, and during the last three years of his life was in charge of the construction of the Cathedral of Florence. The design of the famous bell tower is his, and he is said also to have sculptured some of the reliefs with which it is adorned. Rising even above the church's great dome, it is visible for miles, a fitting and lovely monument to one of the city's greatest artists.

During the same years when Giotto was painting the frescoes in the Arena Chapel, Dante Alighieri, greatest of all Italian poets and Giotto's almost exact contemporary, was working on his masterpiece, the *Divine Comedy*. The long poem is an epic account of Dante's imaginary journey through Purgatory and the Inferno, with the guidance of the great Roman poet Vergil, and finally to Paradise, where he meets his beloved Beatrice. But it is also far more than a journey into fantasy. Enlivened by character sketches of friends and enemies, the latter suffering the tortures of the damned, the powerful verses describe a cosmic pattern of the world, God, and the fate of man. Dante was an embittered Florentine aristocrat forced into a life of exile because of his political loyalties, and Giotto was of peasant family, country born. Yet they almost surely knew each other. The painter is praised in the poet's verses, and the poet's distinguished aquiline profile appears in a painting ascribed to the artist. Though there were differences between them, they had much in common. Dante's works established the native Italian of Tuscany as the language of literature and of the future, the living, spoken tongue, rather than Latin, known only to the Schoolmen. In the same way Giotto painted in an earthy style that was universally understandable rather than in terms of esoteric symbolism meaningful only to the initiated.

Through a life of poverty and service, St. Francis had brought faith and hope into the lives of men. He envisioned the unity of nature as a gift and a manifestation of God, and of man's relation not only to his fellowman but also to the divine. A century later Dante and Giotto shared St. Francis' inspired concept of "the community of creation with the Creator." Dante's poetry showed his countrymen the beauty of the natural world around them, as well as its significance as the expression of a divine plan. Both also had St. Francis' feeling for the divinity in man. It is this spirit which ennobles Dante's verses and Giotto's painting, and suggests the more than earthly significance of earthly life and experience.

The Bell Tower, Designed by Giotto, Rising Above the Cathedral of Florence

IX THE ASCENDANCY OF FLANDERS AND BURGUNDY

The fourteenth century saw the devastation of much of Europe. The horrors of the plague were added to those of war, so that when the Italian poet Petrarch visited France shortly after the middle of the century he could not believe what he saw. Instead of the rich and prosperous kingdom that he remembered, "nothing presented itself to my eyes," he wrote, "but fearful solitude and extreme poverty, uncultivated land and houses in ruins. Even about Paris there were everywhere signs of fire and destruction. The streets were deserted; the roads overgrown with weeds." Wandering bands of brigands terrorized the countryside. The Hundred Years' War, which had seen the destruction of French chivalry before the might of English archers at Crécy and Poitiers, dragged on but intermittently because of the exhaustion of both the French and English after the death of that mighty warrior, Edward, the Black Prince. There were revolts of the peasantry in both countries. All Christendom was shaken by the retreat of the papacy to Avignon in the south of France in what has been called the Babylonian Captivity, and scandalized by the Great Schism that followed, during which rival popes fought for power.

Yet life somehow went on. There were parts of Europe that escaped destruction and even prospered. By the end of the fourteenth century the towns and cities on the coasts and along the waterways of Flanders, today the Netherlands, Belgium, and the northwest corner of France, were flourishing. The weakening of the power of kings under the burdens of war made it possible for the burghers to increase the strength of the communes. Trade went on despite and even because of war, and the comparative stability and security of city life attracted refugees from the ravaged countryside.

In 1361 the Duchy of Burgundy escheated to the crown for lack of an heir. Two years later the ineffectual King John II of France, who much preferred luxurious captivity in England to the rigors of ruling his own disturbed kingdom, awarded the dukedom to his fourth son. Thus the ambitious Philip the Bold became master of a fertile territory, famous for its vineyards, lying on both sides of the Rhone in eastern France bordering Switzerland. Philip's astute elder brother, the Dauphin Charles, acting as regent for his absent father, arranged a marriage between Philip and Margaret, daughter and heiress of the last Count of Flanders. In this way, that rich and populous area was kept from the hands of the English, and the Duke of Burgundy came to control one of the most prosperous parts of the continent.

During the continuance of the Hundred Years' War by Henry V, whose stunning victory against overwhelming numbers at Agincourt in October of 1415 led to his being declared regent of France and heir to the French throne, John the Fearless, who had succeeded his father, was an ally of the English. He and his son, Philip the Good, enlarged their possessions by purchase and astute diplomacy. Their increase in power troubled the kings of France, for the Dukes of Burgundy were among the most splendid rulers in Europe, monarchs in all but name. Duke Charles the Bold determined to rectify this lack by persuading the Emperor to crown him king. But the Duke's rash adventures resulted in his death in 1477 at the hands of Swiss pikemen as he led a charge of mounted chivalry at Nancy in eastern France. His daughter Mary was married to Maximilian, the future emperor. This kept the Burgundian Flemish territories intact and placed them in the possession of the Empire, though the French portion of the duchy was seized by the King of France.

In spite of the disorders of the fifteenth century, which finally saw the English driven from France, largely through the inspired leadership of Joan of Arc, the domains of the Dukes of Burgundy flourished. As the riches of the Flemish cities increased, the ports of Bruges and Antwerp joined Venice, Genoa, and Lübeck as the most active in the West. Flemish cities became centers of finance, with busy offices of the representatives of the great banking houses of Europe. The French word for stock exchange, *bourse,* is derived from the name of the van der Bourse family, whose house

The Chronicles of Hainault, *Master of Girart de Roussillon. Presentation of a volume to Philip the Good, Duke of Burgundy, Flemish, mid-15th century. Bibliothèque Royale, Brussels. Copyright A. C. L., Bruxelles*

in Bruges was a meeting place for Italian and Flemish merchants. In Antwerp in 1460 the first international bourse was established, and in 1489 at Malines the first international postal service was started.

Eager for fame and inspired to outdo their cousins, the kings of France, the Dukes were among the most generous patrons of the arts that the world has seen. The rich burghers, citizens of their Flemish possessions, followed their example. Churches and monasteries, and the houses of merchants as well as the palaces of princes, became treasuries of works of art.

The height of Burgundian power and splendor came under the nearly half century of the reign of Philip the Good (1419–1467). But there had been a centuries-old artistic tradition in the Netherlands that supplied a foundation of well-established guilds to the flowering of Flemish art of the fifteenth century. The cities of the valley of the

Meuse had long been famous for their skill in the production of works of art in metal. The very word *dinanderie*, used for the handsome lecterns, fonts, candlesticks and other such objects made of brass, chiefly for church usage, from the thirteenth century on, is derived from the name of the Flemish city of Dinant. The goldsmith Renier, whose superb font, now in the Church of St.-Barthélemy in Liège, was commissioned early in the twelfth century, came from Huy, a few miles up the river. The area had been famous also for its enamel work, and shrines and chalices, reliquaries and ewers of Mosan craftsmanship were to be found in churches and monasteries all over Europe.

Philip the Good kept artists on his payroll. He surrounded himself with painters, sculptors, architects, and musicians, as well as jurists, poets, historians, financiers, and soldiers. The ducal libraries were famous. Tournai and Brussels were noted for weaving, and the name of the southern Flemish city of Arras became, in common usage, synonymous with tapestry. Perhaps the very uncertainty of life in a disrupted era led men to even more lavish expenditures. Court costumes were the most fashionable and the richest in Europe, and court life was made up of a constant round of musical and theatrical entertainments, tournaments, receptions for illustrious visitors, celebrations, and feasts. On all such occasions the small, slender figure of the Great Duke of the West stood apart. Clad usually in black, with an elaborate headdress, he wore the collar and pendant of the Order of the Golden Fleece, the knightly fraternity open only to royalty and the highest nobility, which he had instituted at the time of his marriage to Isabella of Portugal. The Burgundian court was famous for its formality, and its ceremony was stage-managed with imagination and theatrical precision. The Duke dined apart, waited on by noblemen with foods of great rarity, carried into his presence in procession, and elaborately served in vessels of gold, to the music of lutes and viols. Wherever he went he was accompanied by an honor guard of aristocrats, whose butterflylike brilliance of costume set off the sober richness of his own garb. He chose his ministers with care, and raised a number of commoners to the highest rank because of their ability. Despite the troubled times, both Burgundy and Flanders were better ruled than most of Europe during the period. The arts prospered along with commerce, and Flemish works of art were sought after and found their way into collections of churches and princes far and wide,

as had the earlier works of the Mosan metalworkers and enamelists.

The international flavor of the Burgundian court made it a major center of the arts. Influences from Italy, Germany, France, and the Netherlands met to produce what has been called the International Style, the last phase of medieval art that appeared throughout Europe during the fifteenth century. The single most delightful example of it was produced by painters at the Burgundian court for the Duke's younger brother. A book of hours called *Les Très Riches Heures du Duc de Berry,* because of the extraordinary luxury of its illuminations, became the masterpiece of his large library.

Jean, Duke of Berry, was a far from admirable character. But in an age when princes vied with one another in the richness of their artistic treasures, he must be acknowledged as the equal of his brother of Burgundy. *Les Très Riches Heures* was made at his order by Flemish miniaturists, Pol, Hennequin, and Hermann of Limbourg. These three brothers went to the Burgundian court about 1415 with their uncle, who had just been appointed painter to the Duke. Completed just before Berry's death in 1416, the manuscript is the climax of the art of medieval miniature painting. Since it was a book of private prayers for each day of the year, its illustrations show the seasons with their appropriate activities. January has the elderly Duke entertaining at a banquet. Wearing a figured robe and a fur hat, he is seated in front of a large fireplace, protected by a screen from the direct heat. In front of him is a table covered with dishes of food from which his gorgeously appareled guests help themselves, while two tiny dogs, hardly larger than weasels, run about on the tabletop and snatch such tidbits as may remain on the plates. To the left, a servant pours wine from an elaborate flagon, and in the foreground, another feeds one of the Duke's graceful coursing hounds. The back wall is hung with a tapestry showing long ranks of mounted knights in combat before a city. The tapestry is so faithfully recorded by the miniaturist that we can identify it as one listed in the Duke's inventories as having been woven at Arras.

The scene could not be in greater contrast to that which illustrates February. Instead of courtly comfort and elegance, here is life among peasants. The sheep huddle in their fold and a girl hurries back toward the farmhouse, blowing on her cold fingers, while in the distance a man chops the lord's firewood which another carries away on the back of a donkey, plodding through the snow toward a

January, *from* Les Très Riches Heures du Duc de Berry, *1413–1416, Pol, Hennequin, and Hermann of Limbourg. Musée Condé, Chantilly, France*

February, *from* Les Très Riches Heures du Duc de Berry, *the Limbourg Brothers*

distant village. Magpies scratch for grain in the barnyard, and inside the peasant's house three figures warm themselves before the welcome heat of a fire whose smoke drifts upward from the slender chimney. The sky is gray, the woods bare, and on a bench in the farmyard, protected by its neat wattled fence, the beeskips wear icy caps. It is the first snow scene in Western art. Despite its tiny scale, we shiver with cold, so completely do the painters convey the bitter chill of winter in northern Europe.

Les Très Riches Heures contain all the labors of the months, familiar from details of cathedral sculptures and windows, but in a new, more elaborate form. They are realized to the last detail, yet each carefully observed and recorded element falls into place as a part of a larger whole. A gaily dressed party of lords and ladies ride out to the hunt, falcons at their wrists, on mettlesome horses with stylish trappings, in celebration of the month of August. October shows a bright, sunny day, with peasants harrowing and sowing winter wheat, while blackbirds and magpies help themselves to the newly scattered grain. The freshly seeded field beyond is protected from similar depredations by bits of white rag tied to strings, and by a scarecrow in the form of an archer with bow bent. Beyond flows the Seine, with tiny figures promenading along the quay bordering the farther bank, much as today. Above them rise the towers of the

August, *from* Les Très Riches Heures du Duc de Berry, *the Limbourg Brothers*

October, *from* Les Très Riches Heures du Duc de Berry, *the Limbourg Brothers*

Louvre, the great Gothic castle of the kings of France in Paris as it looked in the high Middle Ages before being rebuilt in later centuries into the tremendous palace so famous as one of the world's great museums.

In the later Middle Ages the cities of Flanders were the rivals of any in Europe. With the founding of its famous university in 1425, Louvain became not only a commercial center but the cultural center of the Netherlands. Its late Gothic Town Hall, built from 1447 to 1463 as a proud symbol of its preeminence, remains as a reminder not only of its past glories but also of the power achieved

Town Hall, Louvain, Belgium, 1447–1463

by the cities during the period.

Ghent, today a lovely relic of the past bypassed by time since the silting up of its harbor brought its prosperity to an end, was as large as Paris. The handsome Gothic Church of St. Bavo there possesses the greatest masterpiece of Flemish art, so famous that it has long been known simply as "the Ghent Altarpiece." The painter, who completed it in 1432, was Jan van Eyck. He was so admired by Philip the Good that the Duke not only commis-

sioned many works from him but also sent him on such important diplomatic missions as that to Portugal in 1428 and 1429 to arrange the Duke's marriage to the princess Isabella.

The altar is large and elaborate, consisting of twelve separate panels, arranged in two tiers, the four on each side hinged to fold back across the central four. When closed, the Annunciation appears at the top. Below, painted in shades of gray to look like sculpture, stand St. John the Baptist with the Lamb of God, and St. John the Evangelist with the serpent in the cup. On either side of the saints kneel the donors of the altar, Jodicus Vyt and his wife, in pious adoration. The Annunciation takes place in an upper room of a

The Ghent Altarpiece open, Hubert and Jan van Eyck, finished 1432, Panel 1' 3" × 14' 5", Church of St. Bavo, Ghent, Belgium. Copyright A. C. L., Bruxelles

Flemish town house such as the Vyts must have lived in, with a view of the city seen through the window. The elaborate folds of the robes of both the Virgin and the angel are not only decorative but expressive. Above, Old Testament prophets look down on the event they foretold.

When the altar is open, the effect is overwhelming. In the center above sits God the Father, richly robed and wearing the triple crown as if in a mystery play. The Virgin sits on His right as Queen of Heaven, and on His left is St. John the Baptist, heavily cloaked and bearded. Flanking the central three panels are two others with angels singing and playing the musical instruments popular in Jan van Eyck's day, when composers of the Netherlands were revolutionizing music just as he and other artists were revolutionizing painting. The magical effects of depth and atmosphere are the result of the then still new manner of painting in glazes of pigment mixed with oil instead of with egg, the technique that has remained basic ever since. Command of the oil medium made possible the subtlety of the two realistic nudes, Adam and Eve, in the outermost panels of the upper tier, and also of the Adoration of the Lamb, in the lower.

Here unfolds the vision of St. John as described in The Revelation. "Lo, a great multitude, which no man could number," of prophets, churchmen, saints, and martyrs, whom "the Lamb . . . shall feed . . ., and shall lead them unto living fountains of waters." The gallant St. Martin rides at the head of the company of the Knights of Christ to the left, while a towering St. Christopher leads the pilgrims from the right. All converge on the altar of the Lamb surrounded by just such typically Flemish angels as those sculptured in stone by Claus de Werve on the tomb of John the Fearless at Dijon, to attend the dead duke and his duchess throughout the ages. Every detail of every figure, every flower and blade of grass, are all recorded with painstaking minuteness. Yet the total result is not that of photographic realism. No camera can photograph a vision. Instead, the very completeness suggests a perfection that cannot be realized in this world but belongs only to a more exalted world "where all time is but an instant."

A contemporary inscription on the frame states that the altar was started by Hubert van Eyck and finished by his brother Jan in 1432. Hubert is recorded as having died in 1426, when he was

Singing Angels, from The Ghent Altarpiece. *Copyright A. C. L., Bruxelles*

buried in the chapel below the famous altarpiece. He was much older than his brother, and nothing of his work is known. As a result scholars disagree about the part each took in the completed whole. There has come to be a general acceptance of the suggestion that originally the entire lower part formed one altarpiece, and the central triptych above, another. The pair of round-topped panels of musical angels might have been originally planned as organ shutters. This would explain the disparity in scale that places the immensely larger figures above and the small below. Thus the only elements added by Jan would be the two powerfully realized nudes, the first of their kind in art, and the composition that appears when the altar is closed.

Whether this theory is true or not, the result has an inner unity that follows the ever-recurring theme of the Redemption of Man. Adam and Eve in their pensive dignity are at once a reminder of God's creation of man in His own image and of the Fall of Man, whose atonement comes through the Word made flesh with the Annunciation, as foretold by prophets and sibyls, and the sacrifice of the blood of the Lamb, and the holy lives and deaths of the saints and martyrs. The entire faith of the Middle Ages is there, orchestrated with incredible fullness of nuance and detail into a grand whole. In a limitless landscape, with the Gothic towers of "the holy city, new Jerusalem" on the horizon, all humanity worships the Lamb. Those who have gone before and those who are to come, all join the choirs of angels in a great hymn of praise and thanksgiving whose visual music echoes silently throughout the altarpiece.

X THE END OF AN EPOCH

The greatest Italian painter of the generation, next to Giotto, was a Sienese, Duccio di Buoninsegna. Three years after Giotto had finished his great frescoes in the Arena Chapel in Padua, Duccio began work on an immense altarpiece for the cathedral of his native city. In a panel almost seven feet high the Virgin is enthroned in majesty as Queen

Angel Announcing Her Forthcoming Death to the Virgin, *Duccio, from the* Maestà Altarpiece

Madonna Enthroned, *Duccio, Central Section of the* Maestà Altarpiece, 1308–1311, Panel, 6′ 10½″ high. *Museum of the Cathedral of Siena*

of Heaven, surrounded by adoring angels. Despite its size, and the grandeur of its simple design, the subject is interpreted with the softness and grace of line that are typically Sienese. Where Giotto's figures stand out in classical solidity like the sculptures of Niccolo Pisano, Duccio's have a delicacy of sinuous line that is essentially Gothic. Yet in the many small panels included in the altarpiece are details closely observed from nature, like the donkeys in the scene of *Christ Entering Jerusalem.* In the *Annunciation to the Virgin of Her Forth-*

coming Death the angel enters an architectural interior which, for the first time in the history of Western art, actually encloses the figures instead of merely forming a background. Yet Duccio's is an otherworldly art. It envisions things of the spirit. Even when he portrays the crucifixion, as on the little altar painted for a private chapel in somebody's house, and now in the Boston Museum, the cruelty and the horror of the event are transformed by the artist's gentleness from tragedy into pathos.

In 1311, Duccio's *Madonna in Majesty* was finished after three years of work. "On the day it was carried to the cathedral," a contemporary chronicler wrote, "the shops were shut, and the bishop conducted a great and devout company of priests and friars in solemn procession, accompanied . . . by all the officers of the commune, and all the people . . . . One after another the worthiest with lighted candles in their hands took places near the picture, and behind came the women and children with great devotion. And they accompanied the said picture up to the cathedral, making the procession around the square, . . . all the bells ringing joyously out of reverence for so noble a picture as this. And this picture Duccio . . . the painter made. . . . And all that day they stood in prayer with great almsgiving for poor persons, praying God and His Mother, who is our advocate, to defend us by their infinite mercy from every adversity and all evil, and keep us from the hands of traitors and of the enemies of Siena."

The celebration of the completion and installation of Duccio's great altarpiece in the Cathedral of Siena was one of the last triumphs of medieval art in Italy. A century later a new era was born in Florence, which was to follow the lead of Giotto, and the last vestiges of the Middle Ages were soon to vanish. In Giotto's grasp of the realities of form, and in the carefully recorded elements of the world of nature and of man in the miniatures of *Les Très Riches Heures du Duc de Berry,* and in the paintings of Jan van Eyck and his followers, we can see the evidence of a changing world. Increasingly men lowered their gaze from things celestial and eternal to things of this world, until it, instead of the world of the spirit, became for them, as for us, the real world.

The Middle Ages waned rapidly in Italy but lingered on in northern Europe. Their final flowering can be seen in the paintings and sculptures of Flemish artists and those influenced by their work, and in the tapestries woven in the Netherlands and in France. Perhaps the greatest of the latter is the unicorn series, five of which were produced for Anne of Brittany in celebration of her marriage to Louis XII in January, 1499. Two others were added when Francis I married Anne's daughter in 1514. For centuries they belonged to the family of Rochefoucauld, one of whom was the godfather of King Francis. During the French Revolution the royal insignia were hacked out of their upper portions and they are said to have been used to keep potatoes from freezing. Yet somehow they survived to become the pride of the collection in The Cloisters in New York.

They tell the story of the hunt of the unicorn, the fabulous beast that could be caught only by a maiden. For the Middle Ages the story became an allegory of the Incarnation, the unicorn becoming a symbol of Christ, the maiden of the Virgin, and the hunter of Gabriel, the angel of the Annunciation.

By the fifteenth century the story had taken on additional meaning as an allegory of courtly love, the elaborate ritual by which a knight dedicated his life to a lady and became her champion. This theme also runs through the series, and Louis' courtship of Anne is suggested by their initials, mottoes, and devices that constantly reappear. In the first tapestry the huntsmen start out with their dogs leashed and led by trainers. They walk through a landscape of trees and flowers, until

The Crucifixion, *Duccio, Central Panel of a Small Triptych. Courtesy, Museum of Fine Arts, Boston. Grant Walker and Charles Potter Kling Funds*

Christ Entering Jerusalem, *Duccio, from the* Maestà
Altarpiece

1. THE START OF THE HUNT

2. THE UNICORN AT THE FOUNTAIN

3. THE UNICORN TRIES TO ESCAPE

4. THE UNICORN DEFENDS HIMSELF

5. THE CAPTURE OF THE UNICORN
(*Fragments*)

6. THE UNICORN IS BROUGHT TO THE CASTLE

7. THE UNICORN IN CAPTIVITY

The Unicorn Tapestries: Detail of the Fourth Tapestry. The Metropolitan Museum of Art, New York, The Cloisters Collection, Gift of John D. Rockfeller, Jr., 1937

they come, in the second tapestry, to a fountain in the forest. There all the animals wait while the unicorn dips his purifying horn into the stream that flows from the fountain, a symbol of the water of eternal life. In the third, the hunters surround the fountain and attack the unicorn, but he is invincible, and in the fourth, fights back valiantly and effectively. In the fifth, the maiden subdues him, and in the sixth, he is wounded and brought back to the castle, under the watchful eye of King Louis and Queen Anne. In the seventh he rests, wounded but unsuffering, in a meadow carpeted with flowers, within a circular enclosure, the enclosed gar-

The Unicorn Tapestries: The Metropolitan Museum of Art, New York, The Cloisters Collection, Gift of John D. Rockefeller, Jr., 1, 2, 3, 4, 6, 7, 1937; 5, 1938

den of Mary's virginity. He is tied with a golden chain, a symbol of marriage, to a tree bearing pomegranates, symbols of fertility. Thus he stands both for the risen Christ and also for the consummation of Anne's marriage to King Louis.

Despite the complicated allegory, so typical of the later Middle Ages, the story is told with great simplicity and drama. Every square inch is full of details of plants and animals and birds, rendered with such accuracy as to be immediately identifiable. Though there has been some fading, the colors are amazingly fresh, and the effect of the series is one of great richness. The compositions are clear, and the action bold, so that the multiplication of fascinating and lively detail remains subordinated to the whole. The anonymous artist who designed them created not only courtly decorations, with a subtle and complex compliment to the King and Queen, but also unforgettable works of art.

The Middle Ages ended not with a sense of triumph but with a sense of tragedy. The breakdown of moral leadership with the decay of the church during the Great Schism brought with it fears and doubts that were to lead to the Reformation, and to the religious wars and persecutions and intolerance of the sixteenth and seventeenth centuries. The Dance of Death was everywhere. In paintings on the walls of houses and churches and in series of popular woodcuts, the posturing, grimacing skeleton of Death seized his victims, rich and poor, layman and clergyman, pope and peasant. Where the artists of the Romanesque and earlier Gothic periods represented Christ as triumphant, those of the later Middle Ages show Him suffering and bleeding, His body lacerated and torn. The serene and smiling Virgin of the High Gothic is replaced by the tragic Late Gothic Madonna sorrowing over the body of her Son.

Sometime shortly after the middle of the fifteenth century an unknown master gave perhaps the finest expression in all art to this recurrent theme of the later Middle Ages. One of the greatest of French works, it was painted for a church in Villeneuve, across the Rhône from the papal city of Avignon. The figures of the Virgin, St. John, and St. Mary Magdalene are isolated against the infinite emptiness of a gold background. Across His mother's dark robe Christ's corpse lies, limp and angular. The pure white of the loincloth emphasizes the marks of suffering on His body. To the left, the unknown priestly donor kneels in silent devotion. The five figures are frozen in attitudes of grief

The Dance of Death, Detail of a 15th-century Mural Painting, Abbey of La Chaise-Dieu, France. Archives Photographiques — Paris

in a composition so simple and so expressive in its contrast of cool dark tones with silvery white that it rises above tragedy to a somber but grand serenity.

Like the unknown master of the tenth century who sculptured the tragic crucifix for Archbishop Gero in the Cathedral of Cologne, the greatest artists of the later Middle Ages had the ability so to sublimate sorrow. Through pious symbolism they gave meaning and dignity to human life, no matter what suffering it might bring. Yet the single most compelling ideal of the medieval world remains its triumphant vision of the unity of man and the universe, quickened by the conviction of a transcendent pattern and purpose to all existence. This vision is most powerfully expressed in the great Gothic cathedrals that remain the crowning achievement of a long and richly varied epoch. We find it in Chartres, among the golden wheat fields of the Beauce; in Paris, on its ancient island in the Seine; in Amiens, soaring high above the earthbound gray city; in Rheims, where the kings of France were crowned. We find it in Sens and Senlis and Noyon, in Laon on its lofty citadel, and in all the other cathedrals scattered across France and Germany, westward beyond the Channel in England, northward in Scandinavia, southward in Spain and Italy. Each is "a mirror of the universe" seen as an organic unity of God, of nature, and of man, living harmoniously to the rhythms of the changing seasons, of the canonical year rung out in church bells for daily devotions, and of the constantly renewing cycle of human life from birth to death. The great cathedrals stand as the noblest monument to the Middle Ages, the expression of their most elevated hope and faith. In their glorious affirmation, they are a fitting climax to the troubled centuries that went before. They are eloquent memorials to the age that created them, and remain in our own godless times inspiring reminders of the mystery of life and of the infinite potentiality of man.

The Avignon Pietà, ca. 1470, Southern French Master, Panel, 5' 4" × 7' 2". The Louvre, Paris

CHRONOLOGICAL TABLE
OF DATES AND EVENTS

DURING THE FOURTH CENTURY: Christianity becomes the religion of the Roman Empire; the barbarian tribes begin to invade the Empire; the capital is shifted from Rome to Constantinople.

312: Constantine the Great defeats Maxentius to become the master of Rome.

324: The Empire reunited, Constantine starts the construction of Old St. Peter's, dedicated in 326, but finally completed only after his death.

325: Constantine calls the first worldwide church council at Nicaea in Asia Minor.

330: Constantinople becomes the capital of the Roman Empire.

337: Constantine dies, is succeeded by his three sons.

376: The Visigoths cross the Danube and invade the Balkans, defeating the footsoldiers of the Emperor Valens with their cavalry, a beginning of the technique of medieval warfare.

396: St. Augustine becomes Bishop of Hippo in North Africa, where he writes his autobiography, entitled *Confessions* (398), and *The City of God* (426).

DURING THE FIFTH CENTURY: The downfall of the Roman Empire of the West; the decline of Rome; and the rise of the Franks.

ca. 400: St. Jerome completes the Vulgate, the standard Latin translation of the Bible.

ca. 406: Gaul is overrun by the barbarian tribes of the Vandals, Suevi, Alans, and Burgundians.

407: Roman troops evacuate Britain, leaving the province open to attack by Picts, Saxons, and other invaders.

410: Alaric the Goth sacks Rome.

419: The Visigothic kingdom of Toulouse is established within the Empire.

429: The Vandals invade North Africa from Spain.

432: St. Patrick's mission to Ireland begins.

440–461: Leo the Great reigns as the first great pope.

ca. 450: The tomb of Galla Placidia is constructed in Ravenna.

450: Attila leads the Huns to invade the Empire; is turned back from Rome in 452.

455: The Vandals sack Rome.

457: Venice is founded on sandbars off the Adriatic coast by refugees from the ravages of the invading Huns.

476: The barbarian chief, Odoacer, deposes Romulus Augustulus, the last Emperor of the West.

481: Clovis becomes King of the Salian Franks.

489–526: Theodoric the Great, King of the Ostrogoths (489–493), rules in Italy from 493 to 526.

496: Clovis, King of the Franks, is converted to Christianity.

DURING THE SIXTH CENTURY: The start of the First Golden Age of Constantinople; the growth of monasteries; the beginning of the flowering of Celtic art.

507: Clovis makes Paris his capital and conquers Aquitaine, forcing the Visigoths into Spain, where they establish a kingdom. On the death of Clovis in 511, his kingdom is divided among his sons.

523: Boethius writes his *Consolation of Philosophy* while imprisoned by Theodoric.

527–565: The reign of the Emperor Justinian marks the beginning of the First Golden Age of Byzantine art.

529: St. Benedict founds the monastery of Monte Cassino and establishes his famous monastic Rule.

532–537: The Cathedral of St. Sophia is constructed in Constantinople.

533–534: Belisarius reconquers North Africa for Justinian.

535–540: Belisarius and Byzantine forces reconquer much of Italy. Rome is largely ruined and reduced to one tenth its former population.

540: The Exarchate is established in Ravenna, a source of Byzantine artistic influence in Italy.

ca. 547: Mosaics of the Emperor Justinian and the Empress Theodora are completed in the Church of S. Vitale, Ravenna.

559: Slavs, Avars, and Persians advance to gates of Constantinople.

563: St. Columba from Ireland founds a monastery on the island of Iona off the coast of Scotland.

568: The Lombards invade Italy.

570: Mohammed is born in Mecca.

ca. 576: St. Gregory of Tours begins his *History of the Franks*.

590–604: Gregory the Great is the first monk to become Pope.

596: St. Augustine, sent on a mission to England, establishes his see at Canterbury.

DURING THE SEVENTH CENTURY: The rise of Moslem power.

622: Mohammed's flight to Medina (the Hejira) begins the Moslem era.

632: Mohammed dies; is succeeded by Abu Bakr, the first Caliph.

634–641: The Arabs overrun Asia Minor, in 647 invade Africa, and in 648 take Cyprus.

661: The Caliphate is established in Damascus.

673–678: The Arabs blockade Constantinople for five years, but their attacks are repulsed by the use of Greek fire.

679: The Bulgars press into the Empire.

ca. 670: Caedmon, the earliest known English lyric poet, translates the Scriptures into Anglo-Saxon verse.

DURING THE EIGHTH CENTURY: Charlemagne unifies the West under his rule, and fosters the revival of classical learning and promotes education; the Moslems invade Spain.

711: Moslem forces from North Africa overthrow the Visigothic kingdom, and reach the Pyrenees by 719.

716: St. Boniface leaves England on his first mission to Germany.

717: The Emperor Leo successfully defends Constantinople from Moslem attack.

ca. 725: *Beowulf*, the great Anglo-Saxon epic, is composed.

731: The Venerable Bede, the father of English history, completes his *Ecclesiastical History of England*.

732: Charles Martel defeats the Moslems at Tours, their farthest penetration into Europe.

751: Pepin the Short, King of the Franks, establishes the Carolingian dynasty. The capture of Ravenna by the Lombards ends Byzantine power in Italy.

756: Abdurrahman founds the Ommiad dynasty at Cordova in Spain.

768: Charlemagne (742–814) becomes King of the Franks. In 773 he invades Italy and becomes King of the Lombards, and extends his rule to Dalmatia and Corsica.

778: Frankish armies are defeated at the Pass of Roncesvalles in the Pyrenees by the Moslems, an event commemorated in the legendary *Song of Roland,* the epic of the Franks, composed ca. 1100.

ca. 781: Charlemagne invites the scholarly churchman Alcuin from England to establish imperial schools.

785: Charlemagne finally conquers and converts the Saxons.

785–809: Harun al-Rashid, one of the greatest Abbasside Caliphs of Baghdad, rules; famous as a character in *The Arabian Nights*.

786–987: The Mosque of Cordova is constructed and enlarged.

793–804: Charlemagne's Palatine Chapel at Aachen is constructed.

DURING THE NINTH CENTURY: The division of the Carolingian empire; the invasions of the Vikings; and the beginning of the Second Golden Age of Byzantine art, which lasts until the eleventh century.

800: Charlemagne is crowned Emperor in Rome by Pope Leo III.

813–833: The reign of Mamun the Great marks the height of the Caliphate of Baghdad.

814: Louis the Pious succeeds Charlemagne as Emperor.

ca. 830: The Utrecht Psalter is illuminated, probably at Rheims.

867–886: The reign of Basil I marks a height of Byzantine power.

871–899: The reign of Alfred the Great, King of the West Saxons, marks the beginning of a consolidation of England, and of English literature.

886: The Norsemen attack Paris.

DURING THE TENTH CENTURY: The beginning of the Holy Roman Empire; the rise of feudalism with the collapse of the Carolingian empire.

910: The Abbey of Cluny is founded.

911: Rollo the Norseman is granted the Duchy of Normandy by the Emperor Charles III.

912–961: The reign of Abdurrahman III marks the height of Arab power in Spain, where Cordova is the greatest cultural center in Europe.

962: King Otto I of Germany is crowned Emperor of the West, the revival of the Holy Roman Empire.

ca. 980: The great crucifix in the Cathedral of Cologne is completed for Archbishop Gero.

986: Eric the Red establishes a Norse colony in Greenland.

987: Hugh Capet is elected King of France, the first of the Capetian dynasty.

989: Prince Vladimir of Russia is converted to Eastern Christianity.

999–1003: The great scholar and teacher Gerbert of Aurillac becomes Pope as Sylvester II; starts to restore Rome with the aid of the Emperor Otto.

DURING THE ELEVENTH CENTURY: The height of Romanesque art; the start of the age of pilgrimages; Norman expansion into England and the Mediterranean; the rise of the Seljuk Turks.

ca. 1000: Scandinavia and Hungary are converted to Christianity.

1015: The bronze doors, ordered by Archbishop Bernward, are cast for the Church of St. Michael, Hildesheim.

1016–1035: Canute the Dane rules Norway, Denmark, and England.

ca. 1025: Guido of Arezzo writes his *Micrologus,* a treatise of great influence on medieval music.

1035: William, the future conqueror of England, becomes Duke of Normandy.

1042–1066: The pious Edward the Confessor is King of England.

ca. 1050: An unknown sculptor carves the doorway of the church at Urnes, Norway.

1055: The Seljuk Turks enter Baghdad.

1059: Pope Nicholas II decrees that popes be elected by cardinals.

1061–1091: The Normans conquer Sicily from the Moslems.

1063: Construction begins on the Cathedral of St. Mark in Venice, the largest surviving church of the Second Golden Age of Byzantine art.

1066: William of Normandy defeats Harald the Saxon at Hastings; conquers England.

1078–1124: The Cathedral of Santiago de Compostela is built.

1080–1120: The pilgrimage Church of St.-Sernin at Toulouse is constructed.

ca. 1088: The Third Church at the Abbey of Cluny, larger than Old St. Peter's, is begun by the abbot, St. Hugh.

1093: Construction is begun on the Cathedral of Durham by Bishop William of St. Carileph.

1096: Pope Urban II calls a Council at Clermont in Auvergne to preach the First Crusade.

1096–1099: The First Crusade: the followers of Peter the Hermit and Walter the Penniless are annihilated in Asia Minor; 1097, the Seljuk capital, Nicaea, is taken by the Christian barons; 1099, Godfrey de Bouillon is elected ruler of Jerusalem.

DURING THE TWELFTH CENTURY: The continuation of the Crusades; the growth of towns and of commerce; the development of the wool market; the start of the period of Gothic art.

ca. 1108: Abbot Hellinus commissions Renier of Huy to cast the bronze font for the Church of Notre-Dame-des-Fonts, Liège.

1122: Suger becomes Abbot of St.-Denis.

1130–1135: Gislebertus is at work on the sculptures of the Cathedral of St.-Lazare at Autun.

1140: Suger's new facade of the Abbey of St.-Denis is dedicated, starting the great age of cathedral building.

1144: Suger's Choir of St.-Denis is dedicated, marking the beginning of the Gothic style.

1145: New construction is begun on the Cathedral of Chartres.

1146: St. Bernard preaches the Second Crusade at Vézelay.

1147–1149: The Second Crusade, led by Louis VII of France and the Emperor Conrad III, achieves nothing.

1163: Work is begun on the Cathedral of Notre-Dame in Paris.

ca. 1167: Oxford University is established on the model of the university in Paris.

1170: Thomas à Becket, Archbishop of Canterbury, is murdered by knights of King Henry II.

1180–1223: The reign of Philip II, called Philip Augustus, marks the consolidation of the French monarchy and state.

1187: The Moslems under Saladin capture Jerusalem.

1189–1192: The Third Crusade follows, led by Richard the Lion-Hearted, Philip Augustus, and the Emperor Frederick Barbarossa. Antioch is saved, but Jerusalem remains in the hands of the Moslems.

1198–1216: The pontificate of Innocent III marks the height of the medieval papacy.

1199–1216: John Lackland is King of England.

DURING THE THIRTEENTH CENTURY: The height of Gothic art; the growth of national languages and literatures; the revival of classical art and learning at the court of the Emperor Frederick II; the establishment of universities; the foundation of the Franciscan and Dominican orders of friars; the coming of the Mongols; the final loss of Jerusalem to the Moslems.

1200: Though the University of Paris was in existence earlier, its charter dates from this year. Construction on the Cathedral of Amiens is started at about this time.

1202-1204: The Fourth Crusade, led by Enrico Dandolo, Doge of Venice, and Boniface of Montferrat, never reaches the Holy Land, but captures and sacks Constantinople in 1204.

1208-1229: The Albigensian Crusade, called by Innocent III against heretics in southern France, lays waste the centers of Provençal culture.

1209: The order of Franciscans is founded.

1209: Cambridge University is founded.

1212: The Children's Crusade.

1215: King John of England signs the Magna Carta at Runnymede.

1215-1250: The reign of the Emperor Frederick II makes Sicily and Southern Italy a center of art and culture.

1216: St. Dominic's order of preaching friars is approved by the Pope.

1218-1221: The Fifth Crusade, called by Pope Innocent III, accomplishes nothing.

1220: The Cathedral of Chartres is largely complete. The Mongols first appear in Europe.

1224: The University of Naples is founded by the Emperor Frederick II, the first in Europe with a royal charter.

1226-1270: The reign of Louis IX, St. Louis, marks the golden age of medieval France.

1228-1229: The Sixth Crusade, led by Frederick II, recovers Jerusalem, Nazareth, and Bethlehem by treaty; the Emperor is crowned King of Jerusalem.

ca. 1240: The Mongols invade Russia and hold it in tribute for two centuries.

1244: Moslem mercenaries recapture Jerusalem, which is not to be in Christian hands again except briefly when General Allenby captured it in 1917 during the First World War.

1248-1254: The Seventh Crusade, led by Louis IX of France, ends in massacre and disaster.

1255-1266: Nicolo and Maffeo Polo, Venetian merchants, journey to Central Asia and China.

1258: The Mongols capture and sack Baghdad.

1260: The Cathedral of Chartres is consecrated.

1267-1273: St. Thomas Aquinas writes his *Summa Theologica* to reconcile classical learning and Christian theology.

1270: The Eighth Crusade, led by Louis IX and Edward of England, is the last of the Crusades.

1271-1295: Marco Polo (1254?-1324) accompanies his father and uncle on their second trip to the Far East, spends fifteen years in the service of the Mongol Emperor of China, Kublai Khan, and probably writes his famous account of his travels while in jail in Genoa after his return.

1272-1307: The reign of Edward I is marked by consolidation of English power, reorganization of the legal system, cultural growth, and significant developments toward parliamentary government.

1273: Rudolph is elected Emperor, the beginning of Hapsburg power.

ca. 1285: Cimabue (ca. 1240-1302?) paints the *Madonna Enthroned*, now in the Uffizi Gallery, Florence.

1290-1300: Giotto (1266/7-1337) is at work on the frescoes in the Church of St. Francis at Assisi.

DURING THE FOURTEENTH CENTURY: The Babylonian Captivity and the Great Schism of the papacy; the height of medieval art in Italy; the start of the Hundred Years' War; the Black Death; the Peasants' Revolt.

1302: Philip IV, the Fair, calls together the Estates-General, representatives of the nobles, clergy, and burghers of France.

1305: Clement V, a Frenchman, is elected Pope, settles at Avignon, thus starting the Babylonian Captivity (1309–1376).

1305–1306: Giotto is at work on the Arena Chapel frescoes in Padua.

1308–1311: Duccio (ca. 1255–1319), first great Sienese painter, is at work on the *Madonna Enthroned* for the Cathedral of Siena.

1321: Dante (1265–1321) completes the *Divine Comedy*.

1338: The Hundred Years' War between France and England breaks out.

1346: At Crécy, English bowmen defeat the mounted chivalry of France; artillery may also have been used.

1348–1349: The Black Death ravages Europe.

1348–1353: Boccaccio writes the *Decameron*.

1354: The Ottoman Turks establish themselves in Europe.

1356: Edward, the Black Prince, defeats the French at Poitiers.

1358: The peasants in northern France (called the Jacquerie) revolt.

1363: Philip the Bold becomes Duke of Burgundy.

ca. 1375: In a vernacular poem, *The Vision of William Concerning Piers the Plowman*, William Langland, a country clergyman, expresses for the first time the plight of the poor peasant.

1378–1417: The Great Schism, with rival popes, divides Christendom.

ca. 1380: The first translation of the Bible into English is being made by the followers of John Wycliffe, an ardent reformer of the church.

1381: The Peasants' Revolt in England, led by Jack Straw and Wat Tyler, is brutally repressed by Richard II.

ca. 1387: Geoffrey Chaucer (ca. 1340–1400) begins writing *The Canterbury Tales*.

1394–1460: Prince Henry the Navigator, with his interest in geography and exploration, ushers in an era of discovery.

DURING THE FIFTEENTH CENTURY: The start of the Renaissance in Italy; the age of discovery; the final fall of the Eastern Empire; the Middle Ages has a final flowering in Burgundy and Flanders.

ca. 1410: Andrei Rublev (ca. 1370–1430) completes his *Old Testament Trinity,* a climax of Byzantine painting in Russia.

1413–1416: The Limbourg brothers work on *Les Très Riches Heures du Duc de Berry* at the court of the Duke of Burgundy.

1415: Henry V of England defeats the French at Agincourt. The Reformer John Hus (b. 1369) is condemned and executed by the Council of Constance.

1416–1458: The reign of Alfonso V of Aragon and Naples brings the Renaissance to Southern Italy.

1417: The election of Martin V finally ends the Great Schism.

1419–1467: The reign of Philip the Good marks the height of the power of Burgundy.

1428: St. Joan of Arc leads an army to relieve the siege of Orléans by the English.

1431: St. Joan is tried by an ecclesiastical court and burned for heresy at Rouen.

1432: The Ghent Altarpiece is completed by Jan van Eyck.

1434: Cosimo de' Medici (1389–1464), one of the greatest early patrons of art of the Renaissance, becomes ruler of Florence.

1451: Cristoforo Colombo is born in Genoa.

1453: The Turks capture Constantinople, bringing the Eastern Empire to an end after a thousand years. The Hundred Years' War is finally over.

1455–1485: The War of the Roses finally ends when Henry, Earl of Richmond, first of the Tudors, becomes King of England.

1460: The first international Bourse is established in Antwerp.

1461–1483: The reign of Louis XI is a period of reconstruction and development in France.

1462–1505: Ivan III, the Great, is the first national sovereign of Russia.

1477: The death of Charles the Bold, the last great Duke of Burgundy, while leading a cavalry charge against Swiss pikeman, leaves the King without a rival in France.

1469: The marriage of Isabella of Castile and Ferdinand of Aragon ensures the unification of Christian Spain.

1478–1492: Under Lorenzo de' Medici, called the Magnificent (b. 1449), comes the flowering of the early Renaissance in Florence.

1492: The fall of Granada to the armies of Ferdinand and Isabella drives the Moslems from Spain. Lorenzo the Magnificent dies in Florence. Columbus makes his first voyage to the New World.

ca. 1500: The series of Unicorn Tapestries, begun to celebrate the marriage of Anne of Brittany to Louis XII of France in 1499, is completed ca. 1514 when Anne's daughter marries Francis I, first Renaissance king of France.

BIBLIOGRAPHY

A tremendous amount has been written on the arts of the Middle Ages, but everyone who works in the field is especially indebted to two of the greatest scholars of the last generation, Charles Rufus Morey and Émile Mâle, whose basic works are listed below. Various volumes in the Pelican History of Art series, published by Penguin Books, Inc., cover many phases of medieval art, while each year sees the publication of more books, often generously illustrated. Many books are prohibitively expensive for most persons and therefore must be consulted in libraries, but are worth the effort. Each year also sees the publication in paperback of both classical and new works in the field.

Important manuscripts, such as the Book of Kells and the Utrecht Psalter, have been published in facsimile, while many monographs dealing with specific subjects bring together through their illustrations a wealth of material often impossible to see without extensive travel.

A number of the museums that are particularly rich in medieval art have published excellent catalogs of their collections, among them The Metropolitan Museum of Art, The Cloisters, and The Pierpont Morgan Library in New York, the Cleveland Museum, the Walters Art Gallery in Baltimore, the Victoria and Albert Museum and the British Museum in London, the Louvre in Paris.

The following list of books has been limited to basic works available in English.

When a book is in paperback, that fact has been noted with an asterisk.

GENERAL BACKGROUND

Baynes, Norman H., and Moss, H. St. L. B., eds., *Byzantium: An Introduction to East Roman Civilization.* Oxford University Press, 1949. An excellent source of general information.

Coulton, G. G., *Medieval Panorama.** Meridian Book, The World Publishing Company, 1955.

Fremantle, Anne, *The Age of Belief.** A Mentor Book, New American Library of World Literature, Inc., 1955. A selection from the writings of the major medieval philosophers.

Haskins, Charles Homer, *The Renaissance of the Twelfth Century.* Harvard University Press, 1927.

Heer, Friedrich, *The Medieval World: Europe, 1100–1350.** The World Publishing Company, 1962; A Mentor Book, The New American Library of World Literature, Inc., 1964. An excellent general introduction.

Huizinga, Johan, *The Waning of the Middle Ages.** London: Edward Arnold, Ltd., 1937; A Doubleday Anchor Book, New York, 1954.

Moss, H. St. L. B., *The Birth of the Middle Ages, 395–814.** Oxford University Press, 1935; Oxford Paperback, 1963.

Pirenne, Henri, *Medieval Cities.** Princeton University Press, 1925.

Power, Eileen, *Medieval People.** London: Methuen & Co., Ltd., 1924; A Doubleday Anchor Book, New York, 1954. A re-creation of the lives of six people who lived during the Middle Ages.

Ross, James Bruce, and McLaughlin, Mary Martin, eds., *The Portable Medieval Reader.** The Viking Press, Inc., 1949. A well-chosen anthology.

Shepherd, William R., *Historical Atlas*, 8th rev. ed. Barnes & Noble, Inc., 1956. Invaluable for study of any period.

Wallace-Hadrill, J. M., *The Barbarian West: The Early Middle Ages, A.D. 400–1000.*° London: Hutchinson & Co., Ltd., 1961; Harper Torchbook, New York, 1962.

THE CRUSADES

Joinville, Jean de, and Villehardouin, Geoffrey de, *Chronicles of the Crusades,*° tr. with an intro. by Margaret R. B. Shaw. Penguin Books, Inc., 1963. A translation of the *Chronicles of the Crusades* and *The Life of St. Louis* by contemporary writers.

Runciman, Sir Stephen, *A History of the Crusades*, 3 vols. Cambridge University Press, 1951–1954. A standard work.

Treece, Henry, *The Crusades.*° Random House, Inc., 1962; A Mentor Book, The New American Library of World Literature, Inc., 1964. A shorter and livelier treatment.

GENERAL ART

Arnold, Hugh, *Stained Glass of the Middle Ages in England and France*, new ed. The Macmillan Company, 1940.

Diringer, David, *The Illuminated Book.* London: Faber & Faber, Ltd., 1958.

Holt, Elizabeth G., ed., *Literary Sources of Art History.* Princeton University Press, 1947. An anthology of texts relative to art and artists from the Middle Ages to the eighteenth century.

Janson, H. W., and Janson, D. J. H., *History of Art.* Harry N. Abrams, Inc., 1962. Sections on "Early Christian and Byzantine Art," "Islamic Art," "Early Medieval Art," "Romanesque Art," "Gothic Art," and "'Late Gothic' Painting, Sculpture, and the Graphic Arts."

Mâle, Émile, *Religious Art from the Twelfth to the Eighteenth Century.*° Pantheon Books, Inc., 1949; Noonday Paperback, 1958.

Morey, Charles Rufus, *Christian Art.*° Longmans, Green & Co., Inc., 1935; Norton Paperback, 1958.

——— *Medieval Art.* W. W. Norton & Company, Inc., 1942. The standard scholarly and perceptive treatment of the subject.

Pevsner, Nikolaus, *An Outline of European Architecture* Penguin Books, Inc., 1960. A most useful survey.

White, T. H., *The Bestiary, A Book of Beasts.*° Capricorn Paperbacks, No. 26, G. P. Putnam's Sons, 1960.

EARLY CHRISTIAN AND BYZANTINE ART

Beckwith, John, *The Art of Constantinople*, London: Burns & MacEachern, 1961.

Morey, Charles Rufus, *Early Christian Art*, 2d ed. Princeton University Press, 1953.

Rice, David Talbot, *The Art of Byzantium.* Harry N. Abrams, Inc., 1959. A large, well-illustrated survey by a leading scholar who has treated much the same subject less massively in *° Art of the Byzantine Era* (Frederick A. Praeger, Inc., Publishers, 1963).

Volbach, Wolfgang F., and Hirmer, Max, *Early Christian Art.* Harry N. Abrams, Inc., 1961. Excellent illustrations of the most complete representation of Early Christian objects and monuments available in a single volume.

EARLY MEDIEVAL ART

Beckwith, John, *Early Medieval Art.*° Frederick A. Praeger, Inc., Publishers, 1964. A well-illustrated general survey.

Conant, Kenneth J., *Carolingian and Romanesque Architecture, 800–1200.* Pelican History of Art. Penguin Books, Inc., 1959. A penetrating study by a distinguished architectural historian.

Grabar, André, *Byzantine Painting.* Skira, Inc., Publishers, 1953.

——— and Nordenfalk, Carl, *Early Medieval Painting.* Skira, Inc., Publishers, 1957.

Henry, Françoise, *Irish Art in the Early Christian Period.* London: Methuen & Co., Ltd., 1940.

Hinks, Roger P., *Carolingian Art.*° London: Sedgwick & Jackson, 1935.

Porter, Arthur Kingsley, *The Crosses and Culture of Ireland.* Yale University Press, 1931.

ISLAMIC ART

Dimand, Maurice S., *A Handbook of Muhammedan Art.* The Metropolitan Museum of Art, 1944.

Ettinghausen, Richard, *Arab Painting.* Skira, Inc., Publishers, 1962.

Rivoira, Giovanni T., *Moslem Architecture*, tr. by G. McN. Rushworth. Oxford University Press, 1918.

ROMANESQUE ART

Anthony, Edgar W., *Romanesque Frescoes.* Princeton University Press, 1951.

Grivot, Denis, and Zarnecki, George, *Gislebertus, Sculptor of Autun.* Orion Press, Inc., 1961. Beautifully illustrated study of one of the leading medieval sculptors.

Nordenfalk, Carl, *Romanesque Painting.* Skira, Inc., Publishers, 1958.

Porter, Arthur Kingsley, *Medieval Architecture*, 2 vols. Yale University Press, 1912.

——— *Romanesque Sculpture of the Pilgrimage Roads*, 10 vols. Marshall Jones Company, 1923. One volume of text and nine of illustrations, a major work by a pioneer in the field.

Stenton, Sir Frank Merry, and others, *The Bayeux Tapestry; A Comprehensive Survey.* Longon: Phaidon Press Ltd., 1965.

Swarzenski, Hanns, *Monuments of Romanesque Art.* The University of Chicago Press, 1954.

GOTHIC ART

Abbot Suger on the Abbey Church of St.-Denis and Its Art Treasures, tr. by Erwin Panofsky. Princeton University Press, 1946. A key document in medieval art by an extraordinary man who exerted great influence on the development of Gothic architecture.

Adams, Henry, *Mont-Saint-Michel and Chartres,*° many editions. A fascinating re-creation of the Middle Ages.

Dupont, J., and Gnudi, C., *Gothic Painting.* Skira, Inc., Publishers, 1954.

Evans, Joan, *Art in Medieval France.* Oxford University Press, 1948.

Frankl, Paul, *The Gothic.* Princeton University Press, 1960.

Gimpel, Jean, *The Cathedral Builders.*° Grove Press, Inc., 1961. Good, lively account of the great age of cathedral building.

Katzenellenbogen, Adolf, *The Sculptural Programs of Chartres Cathedral.*° The Johns Hopkins Press, 1959; Norton Paperback, 1964. A detailed study of the sculpture of one of the greatest cathedrals.

Mâle, Émile, *Religious Art in France in the Thirteenth Century.*° E. P. Dutton & Company, Inc., 1913; republished as *The Gothic Image,* Harper Torchbook, 1958. A classic work by a great scholar.

Simson, Otto G. von, *The Gothic Cathedral.*° Pantheon Books, Inc., 1956; Harper Torchbook, 1964. A scholarly study of the origins of Gothic architecture and the medieval concept of order.

Temko, Allan, *Notre-Dame of Paris, The Biography of a Cathedral.*° The Viking Press, Inc., 1952; Compass Book, 1959. An immensely readable account of the history of one of the world's great artistic monuments.

ACKNOWLEDGMENTS

Among those who deserve particular thanks for their contribution to this book are Professor Kenneth J. Conant, who granted the use of his expert reconstruction drawings and plans of Old St. Peter's, Cluny, and other buildings, which are models of imaginative and painstaking scholarship, and Professor Harry Bober, of the Institute of Fine Arts of New York University, for reading the manuscript and giving thoughtful criticism.

Valuable assistance was given by many, including Professors Turpin Bannister, of the University of Illinois; Whitney Stoddard, of Williams College; and Sumner McK. Crosby and George H. Hamilton, of Yale University; Miss Felice Stampfle and John Plummer, of The Pierpont Morgan Library; Miss Marjory Childs and Miss Elizabeth Riegel, of the Museum of Fine Arts, Boston; John A. Pope, Director, and Richard Ettinghausen, of the Freer Gallery of Art, Washington, D.C.; Paul Perrot, Director, Kenneth M. Wilson, and Miss Jane Shadel, of the Corning Museum of Glass, Corning, New York; and John Maxon, Director of the Chicago Art Institute.

The author is also grateful to Miss Erna Aasheim, of the University Museum, Oslo; Jean Adhémar, Director of the Bibliothèque Nationale, Paris; Miss Cathleen Brady, of the Irish Tourist Board, New York; Nicholas Cooper, of the National Buildings Record, London; Necati Delunay, Director of Archaeological Museums, Istanbul; Signora Alberta Fabris, of the Instituto Italiano di Cultura, New York; P. M. M. Guerts, of the Manuscript Section, Utrecht University Library; F. J. E. Hurst, Librarian of Trinity College, Dublin; Georg Kugler, of the Kunsthistorisches Museum, Vienna; Ernest Nash, of the Fototeca di Architettura e Topografica del' Italia Antica, Rome; S. G. Tewari, of the Government Archaeological Survey of India; Roger Vaurs, of the French Embassy Cultural Services, New York; and Harry N. Abrams, Mrs. Barbara Adler, John Canady, Peter Fink, and Chase Horton, all of New York.

Especial thanks are due to the officers of the institutions who allowed the use of objects in their care as illustrations, to their photographic departments, to the national information and tourist agencies, and to the others who assisted in supplying photographs from which the illustrations were selected.

But finally, for constant encouragement, perceptive criticism, and invaluable practical assistance in typing and preparing the manuscript, I am most deeply indebted to my wife.

RICHARD MCLANATHAN

BIOGRAPHY
OF RICHARD McLANATHAN

Born in Massachusetts in 1916, Richard McLanathan went to The Choate School and to Harvard, where, after graduation, he was elected a member of the Society of Fellows and received his doctorate in the History of Art. During more than a decade on the staff of the Museum of Fine Arts in Boston he was Assistant Curator of Paintings, Editor of Publications, Secretary of the Museum, and Curator of Decorative Arts, a department which includes a significant collection of medieval sculpture and other works of art. In 1957 he became Director of the Museum of Art in Utica, New York, to coordinate a four-year building and development program. Since 1961 he has been living in New York City as a writer, lecturer, and consultant on art.

Dr. McLanathan received the Prix de Rome in 1948 and spent a year studying medieval and Renaissance art in Italy and elsewhere in Europe. On later trips he followed the ancient Pilgrimage Roads to Santiago de Compostela in Spain and to Rome, and studied many monuments and collections of art from London to Istanbul.

In 1959 he served as Curator of the Art Exhibit at the American National Exhibition in Moscow for the United States Information Agency, and later traveled as an American Specialist for the State Department to West Germany, Denmark, Poland, and Yugoslavia. He has produced numerous museum publications, was decorative arts editor for *Webster's Unabridged Dictionary*, and is a contributor to the *Encyclopedia of World Art*. His articles have appeared in many periodicals, including *Art News, Antiques, The New York Times*, and the *Atlantic Monthly*, and he is the author of *Images of the Universe*, a book on Leonardo da Vinci.

INDEX

Titles of paintings, sculptures, and literary works are in italics. Page numbers in italics refer to illustrations.